MW00983421

"If you can read only one book this year, read *Don't Start a Side Hustle!* It's like getting a master's degree in living your truth."

—AKBAR SHEIKH,
7-figure coach, speaker, and philanthropist

"*Don't Start a Side Hustle!* is a guide to creating wealth through discipline! Not a 'get rich quick' lesson—instead a handbook of real, everyday work ethics that will help you build wealth and keep it. Read it, and give it to your kids to read!"

—SCOTT McEWEN,
author of the #1 *New York Times*
bestseller *American Sniper*

"Game-changing. Original. A must-read for every hustler out there! Brian's story will motivate you to live an abundant life."

—JON GORDON,
14-time bestselling author of *The Energy Bus*

"The most in-depth and comprehensive look on what it takes to produce your own passivepreneur revolution."

—BRENT SMITH,
private advisor to UHNW clients and lifestyle consultant

"This book is for every entrepreneur that wants to do more than just 'make money.' If you're interested in learning how to make your money *work for you*, this is the book. Stop just being an entrepreneur and learn how to be a passivepreneur!"

—PAUL GETTER,
The Internet Marketing Nerd
and digital marketing agency owner

"Inspirational, motivational, and instructional. Brian Page has created an invaluable resource for entrepreneurs wanting to reclaim their time, create additional streams of income, and achieve personal fulfillment."

—MATT ANDREWS,
venture capitalist, investor, author, and philanthropist

"I know there are a ton of people who are pursuing passive income, or a way out of a nine-to-five day job. Once I saw what Brian was doing, I said, 'This is a game changer!'" **—MIKE DILLARD,**
founder of Richer Every Day

"Brian is the king of cash flow. If you can fog a mirror, you can do this."
—RON LeGRAND,
real estate expert and bestselling author

"Brian's story is on FIRE and will IGNITE anyone to live free and live wealthy, both financially and personally." **—JOHN LEE DUMAS,**
host of *Entrepreneurs on Fire*

"This book will challenge you to rethink what it means to be truly wealthy—not just financially but in every other arena of life."
—TIM STOREY,
acclaimed author, speaker, and life coach

"If you only read one book this year, make it this one. Brian will show you how to radically change the trajectory of your own personal wealth journey. This is a must-read for any aspiring entrepreneur."
—CALEB MADDIX,
influencer and CEO of Apex Holdings

DON'T START A SIDE HUSTLE!

Work Less, Earn More, and Live Free

BRIAN PAGE

HARPERCOLLINS
LEADERSHIP

AN IMPRINT OF HARPERCOLLINS

Published by HarperCollins Leadership, an imprint of HarperCollins Focus LLC.

Any internet addresses, phone numbers, or company or product information printed in this book are offered as a resource and are not intended in any way to be or to imply an endorsement by HarperCollins Leadership, nor does HarperCollins Leadership vouch for the existence, content, or services of these sites, phone numbers, companies, or products beyond the life of this book.

This book is written as a source of information only. The information contained in this book should by no means be considered a substitute for the advice, decisions, or judgment of the reader's professional or financial advisors. All efforts have been made to ensure the accuracy of the information contained in this book as of the date published. The author and the publisher expressly disclaim responsibility for any adverse effects arising from the use or application of the information contained herein.

Illustrations by Sandra Rivero Ortiz
Book design by Aubrey Khan, Neuwirth & Associates, Inc.

ISBN 978-1-4002-3141-6 (eBook)
ISBN 978-1-4002-3140-9 (HC)

Library of Congress Control Number: 2022941874

Printed in the United States of America
22 23 24 25 26 LSC 10 9 8 7 6 5 4 3 2 1

[TO DAD.]
I'M NO TOLKIEN,
BUT THIS IS FOR YOU.

[CONTENTS]

INTRODUCTION

[INTRODUCTION]

"I'M GOING TO GIVE YOU a few minutes to say your goodbyes. When you're ready, I'll come back in the room and turn off the ventilator. We will then let your father rest in peace," the doctor told us gently.

A few hours earlier I had gotten a frantic call from my mom, saying my father had collapsed in his room. I immediately left my house and drove four hours to where they lived. That's a long time to spend on the highway wondering if your father is dead or alive.

When I arrived at the hospital, I found my mom and my sister in the critical care unit, at my dad's bedside. He was in a cramped room hooked up to multiple tubes and monitors. Other than the sound of air being pumped in and out of his lungs, the room was silent.

"He has no brain activity," my mom said in a soft voice. "The machine is keeping him breathing but he hasn't moved at all since we got here." *Surely that's not my dad lying here in front of me*, I thought. I saw his body on the table, but was *he* there?

Months earlier, my dad found several lumps around his neck and armpits and was diagnosed with stage 4 melanoma. The specialists told him the cancer had spread to his internal organs, but they were never clear on how much time he had. A few days before he was taken to the hospital, he told my mother he felt like he was in his last days. Never one to be dramatic, his statement rocked our entire family.

Since the time he was diagnosed I would regularly make the long drive to see him at his house. I noticed his health declining with each visit. During those days at his house we had many conversations about life, the kinds of conversations a son would hope to have with his father. I'm thankful I had that extra time with him.

One conversation stood out to me during those last few months. One night after he took his medication and fell asleep early, my mom told me what they had spoken about the day before I arrived.

She said, "Your dad was really suffering yesterday. He never cries, but yesterday he really broke down. You know what he said to me? He said he wasn't ready to go yet. He told me he never got to do the things he wanted to do with his life.

"Your dad told me that as a boy he wanted to be a pilot and was in love with planes. But his father told him it would never happen and not to bring the idea up again. So your dad never pursued it any further."

I didn't know that about my dad. I assumed he had experienced everything he wanted in his life. If he felt otherwise, he never told us.

Most of my life, my father worked as a pastor. Although he felt called, decades of preaching led to burnout. His next job, far removed from church life, was at a call center for a cable company.

My dad was always the number-one or -two performer in the region for his ability to sell on the phone. He was proud that he could take tons of abuse from callers and still smile through the phone. When irate customers cussed him out and screamed into the phone that their cable went out in the middle of a game, he would politely explain that their service was turned off because they hadn't paid their bill in ninety days.

But he despised the work. Every minute of his day was tracked, even when he needed to run to the bathroom. If he returned even one minute late from his brief lunch break, he was penalized. At the end of each day he would be so exhausted that he'd go straight to his room and collapse on the bed. He'd wake to have dinner a few hours later and then return to bed for the night. The next morning he'd wake up at four to do it all over again.

But by the time he reached his seventies, he had no savings of any kind. That job devoured all his time, energy, and the best years of his life. It was brutal, relentless work. But he did it to support himself and my mother. I respect him immensely for that.

A year before he was diagnosed, I told him, "Dad, I know this job is killing you. I want to help you. I'm gonna get you out of debt and take care of you and mom from now on. Also, I want to buy you a house. You can go ahead and put in your two weeks." He and my mom were shocked.

For the first time in his life, my dad didn't have to work.

They decided to move to a quaint town in the foothills of western South Carolina. They found a four-bedroom ranch in a new-construction neighborhood, and I bought it for them as I'd promised. The house was minutes from a beautiful lake where he could take his boat. Every week he'd be out there with his two dogs, exploring each cove and waterway. He was living his dream. Despite COVID and the lockdowns, it was a good year for him and Mom.

But the decades of soul-crushing work and a lifetime struggling to make ends meet had taken their toll on my father. His body was worn out, his joints were arthritic, and he was always in pain. Although he was now retired, he didn't have the health to stay active and he began to decline quickly.

My father ran out of time. I was angry that he never got to enjoy his retirement years. I was boiling with questions: How was it that he never got ahead financially during his life? Why did he spend all of his time doing what he hated just to collect a paycheck? What other dreams did he not get to experience?

One of my father's steadfast dreams for me had been to get a job. When I was a teenager, I disagreed. I'd seen too many people work at something that made them miserable. Why would I want that? I didn't know what the alternative was, but I knew there had to be a better way.

When discussions of college came up he would say, "You are going to college, son. It's not up for discussion. Get a degree—get any degree and graduate. Just go to college." I wasn't fully sold on the idea but started looking at schools.

This was my thought process when it came to looking at schools: *UNC Wilmington is at the beach? Okay, that one gets a yes.*

This other college is near ski resorts in the mountains? That sounds even better. Let's go to the mountains.

I applied to just one school and six months later I was packing my bags for Appalachian State University. Two years later I was a solid B student, but I still couldn't choose a major—every one of them seemed boring to me. I finally settled on Leisure Studies (yes, it's a major). My dad did say get a degree—any degree, right?

Needless to say, the major was a breeze. So I would get to spend most of my time rock climbing and skiing or exploring the Blue Ridge Parkway. I did not take school too seriously and generally questioned authority. I graduated four and a half years later and got that not-so-useful degree.

Everything I cherished from those years was related to the experiences I had outside of class and much of what I lived then formed my life philosophy today. That philosophy has allowed me to live an extraordinary life, the kind that few people get to experience. I got to travel, live, and do what I wanted nearly all the time. I've rarely needed to work a regular job. I want to explore this theme throughout this book, to inspire you about what's possible and on the path to being time rich.

The principles I will show you will lay the foundation on which you can build true wealth—wealth that can be measured in both dollars and cents as well as minutes and hours. This foundation will allow you to fire your boss if you so choose, because where we're going, we don't need bosses.

First we will calculate the monthly income needed to forever walk away from a job. Next we will identify one or more assets that can be owned, created, or controlled to hit that income target as quickly as possible. Finally we will move on to adding in other passive-income-producing assets that will go to work for us, so we don't have to.

You'll learn practical skills, like how to have laser-sharp focus to do the most you can in the least amount of time allotted. You'll learn big-picture strategies that will help you see your personal path to wealth. We'll discuss how changing your beliefs can help you achieve your goals and the difference between thinking exponentially vs. linearly. I'd like to teach you about vehicles vs. careers, how to make sure you've chosen the right wealth vehicle, and the distinction between experience and expertise.

Finally we will explore the specific income-producing assets "passivepreneurs" use to get them to their destination, many of which may surprise you. We'll move away from ideas like overtime, dollars per hour, paychecks, jobs, and salaries and move toward ideas like wealth vehicles, assets, passive income, cash flow, and discretionary time.

While everyone else works their asses off to earn a living, we will instead live off our assets. Are you ready? Let's get started.

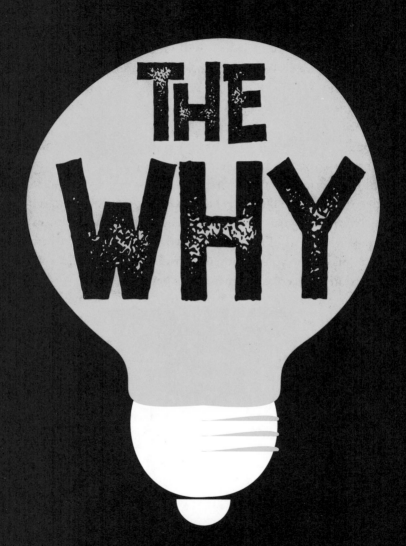

PART I

THE WHY

[1]

A REASON
TO BE RICH

> **PETER GIBBONS:** I don't like my job, and, uh, I don't think I'm gonna go anymore.
>
> **JOANNA:** So you're gonna quit?
>
> **PETER GIBBONS:** Nuh-uh. Not really. Uh . . . I'm just gonna stop going."
>
> **—OFFICE SPACE**

DESPITE BEING THE MOST EDUCATED generations in history, half of all Gen Z and Millennial college graduates are still living at home three years later after getting their diplomas.¹ Toxic work culture, abusive management, employees feeling disrespected, unethical behavior, and a cutthroat corporate culture are fueling a worrisome trend called the antiwork movement. The Reddit subthread r/antiwork, where fed-up employees post screenshots of themselves quitting their jobs, is one of the fastest growing communities on the platform with more than two million users.

A new generation of workers who call themselves "idlers" work just enough not to get fired yet still get a paycheck. In China, a massive movement called *tang ping* ("lying flat") is underway, which rejects the idea of working for a living or contributing to society.[2]

In the COVID era, millions of workers are walking away from their careers in what economists call "the Great Resignation." Businesses are experiencing record levels of turnover as unsatisfied workers jump ship for better opportunities. Although many quit for better pay or benefits, a report published by *MIT Sloan Management Review* found that the biggest single driver of this exodus is a toxic workplace.[3] Low-paid industries like retail, restaurants, and hospitality as well as higher-paid jobs like consulting, software, nursing, and IT are all at crisis levels of understaffing. With so many dissatisfied, it appears work no longer works!

Does working less make people happier? Recent research seems to support this idea. The World Economic Forum studied the relationship between the level of happiness of a country's citizens and average hours worked. The data showed that the five happiest countries in the world are Finland, Denmark, Norway, Iceland, and the Netherlands.[4] On average, workers in these countries put in hundreds of hours less per year than those in other wealthy nations.

Greece, Turkey, Portugal, Hungary, and Japan, on the other hand, work considerably more hours than the average country and are generally less happy overall. The big takeaway from this study is that, with the exception of Israel, countries with the highest levels of happiness are those that work the least.

For decades the typical forty-hour, five-day workweek has been the norm. But this is changing. An increasing number of companies are experimenting with four-day workweeks or workdays with less than six hours. The results are telling. When these companies reduced the number of days or the average hours worked, stress levels decreased. Not only did people feel less stressed, but job satisfaction increased. A larger segment of the population is beginning to reevaluate their relationship with work and the amount of their lives they want to devote to it. Working less is now becoming more mainstream as the trend is accelerating.

A fascinating experiment took place in Japan, a country known for extreme overtime. Hard work is highly prized as a virtue and working oneself to death is a not-uncommon occurrence. Known as (karoshi) which translates to "death from overwork," some have been known to put in seventy-plus-hour weeks until their bodies give out.[5] They suffer chronic health issues and dangerous levels of stress, leading to death.

Microsoft started experimenting with a four-day workweek in 2019 at their Asia headquarters in Japan. Based on their reports, the Japan office experienced a 40 percent boost in productivity with one less day per week in the office.[6] Perhaps working less is not only preferable, but beneficial.

Before we move on, this book is not about "four-hour workweeks," although we will further talk about reducing time at work. This is not a book about anticapitalist ideology. I don't support opting out of society or living in a van down by the river, and eating government cheese, as Matt Foley on *Saturday Night Live* is famous for declaring. I won't be advocating the idea of doing nothing, becoming nomadic, or couch surfing for a living. I'm not for a universal basic income or living off the government teat either. What I am proposing is that we examine our relationship with work. The best way I know to gain clarity is to ask the right questions. Let's begin with what I call the Powerball Question.

Imagine tomorrow you wake up to find that you won the lottery. Imagine it's the Powerball, which sits at $132 million. You wake up, count all those zeros, and realize you are a centimillionaire. The Powerball Question is: Do you go into work today?

I believe if we removed all financial incentives from the equation of work, the majority of us would quit. We say work is about making a difference, being challenged, or some other high ideal, but the truth is most of us go to work for one primary reason: a paycheck. I believe most people, upon winning the lottery, would say, "Take this job and shove it!" I believe they would suddenly find many other better uses of their time—things they never had the time to do, until now.

> Truly I tell you, unless you change and become like little children, you will never enter the kingdom of heaven."
>
> **—MATTHEW 18:4**

As a kid, what did you want to be when you grew up? Likely it was something extraordinary like becoming an astronaut, a ballerina, or president of the United States. Maybe you dreamt of being a superhero or a rock star.

When I was nine, I believed that one day I would be Indiana Jones. I imagined I'd be a whip-carrying, leather jacket–wearing badass archaeologist. My days would be filled with treasure quests and exploring snake-filled tunnels and dodging poison darts. I'd stay one step ahead of the bad guys as I searched for the Holy Grail. Little did I know that archaeologists spend most of their time in research libraries, not looking for treasure.

Like most kids, I believed the possibilities were unlimited. What I wanted to be later in life had nothing to do with making money or even making a living. How I saw myself as a grown-up mirrored what I loved to do for play. I hadn't yet come to understand that there was a "real world" with obligations and coworkers, deadlines and routine. I was years away from resigning myself to the fact that I had to pay rent and student loans and put food on my own table. I had no idea that work would consume the better part of my life and that life itself is a lot of work.

As children, we can't imagine doing anything other than what we most love. So we only dream about what excites us and lights us up. Children never say, "I want to be a corporate drone in middle management with little to no room for advancement in a company that finds me replaceable." Kids can't fathom working sixty-hour weeks, or experiencing existential dread when the alarm clock goes off on Mondays.

Imagine for a moment that you are once again your ten-year-old self. Feel what it was like to be in that little body. Anything is possible. Before your adult sensibilities kick in and shut down this thought experiment, see if you can get a glimpse. Do you remember? How different our lives are now, right? As you read this book, my hope is that it may guide you to creating a life and work that you love.

 Roads? Where we're going, we don't need roads."
            —EMMETT "DOC" BROWN, *Back to the Future*

One of my very favorite movies is *Back to the Future*. At the end of the movie, Marty and his crazy-haired professor, Doc, are in a DeLorean time machine. They pull out of Marty's driveway into a residential street and are about to take off. They will need to hit eighty-eight miles an hour from a dead stop for the time machine to take them to a different year. Right as Doc is about to hit the accelerator, Marty nervously speaks up. "Hey, we better back up. We don't have enough road to get up to eighty-eight miles per hour."

Doc replies, "Roads? Where we're going, we don't need roads."

Where we're going, we don't need jobs. The fact is we won't need bosses, gigs, or vacation time. You can light your punch cards and paychecks on fire, shred your W2s, and chop up the corporate ladder for kindling. While you're at it, you can kick your side hustles to the curb. We won't need any of that where we're going.

[2]

QUESTIONS ARE
SO UNDERRATED

ONE OF MY FAVORITE FINANCIAL advisors is Dave Ramsey. He hosts a no-nonsense financial radio show where he helps people cut up their credit cards and kick their debt addiction. When callers dial in to his show, one of the most common questions they ask is: Should I sell?

"Would you recommend I sell my car and pay off the loan?"

"Should I sell my house or my investment property to pay off my debt?"

"Would you recommend I get out my stocks right now, or sell this widget that I bought?"

Dave usually responds with another question. "If you already had the money in your hand right now from selling [insert what they are considering selling], would you buy it again today?" A light bulb goes off for most callers. When given the opportunity to make a past choice again, but with the life experience and context of today, it's easy to see the right choice.

I'd like to ask you my own version of that question. Imagine if you had back every single minute you've ever spent working. Add in every overtime hour you've ever worked and every decade you've invested in your career. If you had that time back right now to do with as you please, how would you spend it? Would you change anything?

What if we took that question and applied it to the future? If you had every minute from today until the end of your life to spend as you choose—and only as you choose—what would you do?

Giving ourselves a "do-over" allows us to ask hard questions. Would I choose this job or career again? Would I finally do what I've always dreamt of doing with my life? Would I only spend time in pursuit of what I'm passionate about or in the company of those I love? What if work was not a top consideration?

This may seem like an unrealistic thought experiment but stay with me. New ways of seeing the world only emerge by asking ourselves new questions. As Tony Robbins says, "The quality of your life is in direct proportion to the quality of questions you ask."

New questions may even be uncomfortable or on the surface appear unrealistic because they are so novel. Often our brain immediately thinks that it's not possible.

"Brian, I work a full-time job and I'm a parent and a spouse; I have responsibilities. I have no time as it is now."

"I make enough to cover my bills and maybe even have some left over, but I hardly could choose to stop working. I need my job."

'Would you tell me, please, which way I ought to go from here?'

'That depends a good deal on where you want to get to,' said the Cat.

'I don't much care where,' said Alice.

'Then it doesn't matter which way you go.'"

—LEWIS CARROLL,
Alice in Wonderland

The reason we must ask ourselves new questions is because it's only with "blank-slate thinking" that we can craft our lives to be magical. New possibilities can emerge from at least considering what may right now seem impossible.

There is a new class of wealthy people emerging today, a group I call the passivepreneurs. They are financially well to do (think money/income/assets) but also rich in discretionary time. Their lifestyle allows them to be anywhere on the globe they like, with whomever they want to bring along for the ride, and for as long as they want to be there.

Passivepreneurs are not traditional high-income earners like surgeons or attorneys. Neither are they the titans of business who run billion-dollar companies. They don't run tech startups in Silicon Valley or work on Wall Street. They are not trust fund kids who won the "lucky sperm club sweepstakes" and were born into money. They come from diverse backgrounds and education levels and look very different from one another. But the one thing they do all have in common is that they have mastered the art of creating passive income. They live a life of unlimited time, ultimate choice, and true financial freedom.

In this book we will profile many of these individuals and how they differ from the run-of-the-mill "money rich." I'd like to show you how focusing solely on increasing the digits in your bank account is a recipe for disaster because money is but one factor in measuring what it is to be rich. I'd like to show you how becoming a passivepreneur is not only possible but can happen in considerably less time than you may think.

The first thing that you will learn about passivepreneurs is that they all have a financial source from which they can draw. This source is not earned income and it is never a job. Their passive income vehicle (or PIV, as we will refer to it in this book) requires little if any of their direct time to maintain. Their financial source is independent of them; and it feeds them day in and day out, re-gardless of what they do. They do not live to work; their PIVs do that for them.

The highest priority of a passivepreneur is not to hit some arbi-trary dollar amount in the bank, like a million dollars. They aren't chasing a higher salary or a vague idea of "more" money. In fact money is so little of a concern for them that they don't think about it much. They are too busy enjoying life. They have built reliable and redundant sources of cash flow that allow them to have a very different relationship with money than those who have a high net worth but are time bankrupt.

What would you do if you were time rich? Would you go on a three-month tour of Europe and then jump to another continent for the next three? Would you join a martial arts class to get your black belt, become an actor at the local theater, or pursue becoming a master musician? Would you stay home with the kids when they're young? How about going into full-time unpaid ministry, becoming a missionary, or starting a nonprofit? Would you hike the length of the Appalachian Trail and bring no cell phone with you? Would you spend your days anchored in the stunning Charleston harbor while you write your first book, as I'm doing right now?

Think about what life would be like if you no longer had to think about the kind of work you do for money, a life where week-ends were no more exciting than weekdays, because every day of the week was yours. Imagine no one telling you where you have to be or for how long you can be gone. Any of this and more will be open to you when you become a passivepreneur.

FINDING YOUR WHY

I've learned that it's rarely the mechanics of *how* to achieve our dreams that hold us back. "How" is everywhere. A quick Google search will show you how to do nearly anything a human has done before. It's not the *how* that is elusive but the *why*.

It's personal. Your why is unlikely to be my why. You may want to buy a forty-foot blue water sailboat and go single-handing around the globe for the rest of your life. Why? Because your life is about adventure and challenge and taking risks. You may want to volunteer at a homeless outreach nonprofit every day. Why? Because your life is about contributing to others and helping the less fortunate. Those whys are what we must get clear on before we seek out the how.

The reason our deep desire must come before taking any action is because the why is the juice; it's the fuel. Spend some time considering why. The answer to this question has the power to catapult you out of bed in the morning like a kid on Christmas day. Getting clear on your answer will push you to do what's required to make your wildest dreams a reality. Because it won't be easy.

Wait, what? Let me say that again: it won't be easy. If you want to have it all, you must be willing to give it all. This new way of living has a steep price. That's why so few experience it. No-effort results may sell a lot of workout videos, but that is not how life works. The good news is, I'm going to share with you the three-to-five-year plan, and not the three-to-five-decade plan. I'll help you swap the forty- to sixty-hour job for forty to sixty hours of free time. I'll show you how, if you're willing to work your ass off for a short time, you can create results that last a lifetime.

OPPORTUNITY ABOUNDS

[3]

CONSIDER THIS YOUR WAKE-UP CALL

CONSIDER THIS BOOK YOUR WAKE-UP call. My hope is that it will allow you to give up doing the same thing every single day, and every single year, in the hope that one day you'll arrive at a different life. This plan gets you where you want to go much sooner and with plenty of life left in the tank to enjoy the destination when you get there! That's what I want to explore with you. It's possible, not just because I've done it for myself or because the people in this book have done it, but because *anybody* can do it. If you have your why, I'll show you how.

We live in a truly prosperous and abundant time in human history. Only a few decades ago information was difficult to access. There was no internet, no Wikipedia, no YouTube tutorials, no virtual courses. There was no remote learning. An ocean of free content was inconceivable. Today the entire history of human knowledge is available on a device in our pocket!

Imagine going back in time to 1984. You're zapped to Earth in a bolt of lightning like the Terminator. You don't have to be naked in this story, by the way. Onlookers are terrified by your sudden appearance, and a news crew shows up to interview you. You tell them you're from the 2020s. They ask you if there are flying cars. You say, "Next question, please." They probe further. You attempt to give them a picture of what modern-day life is like in the 2020s. What you describe to them (despite no flying cars) sounds like science fiction. You tell them wild tales of the World Wide Web, smartphones, Facebook, and Bitcoin. You avoid any mention of TikTok—their brains may explode.

We don't know how good we have it in our present day, but the average big-haired 1980s citizen would be astounded. It's worth pondering: we have more resources available to us now as individuals than at any other time in human history. Opportunity is not only more abundant than ever, but it's more accessible than ever. You, my friend, have excellent timing.

Right now for little to no money out of pocket a business can be launched in a few hours that has the potential to create mouthwatering levels of wealth. Every day new business opportunities arrive that allow us to earn money from any spot on Earth using only a laptop or a smartphone. Access to asset classes through crowdfunding that were once only available to the rich and connected are plentiful, and an army of inexpensive virtual workers is available at a moment's notice.

 It's really clear that the most precious resource we all have is time."

—STEVE JOBS

The takeaway here is that there has never been a more opportune time for the average person to create passive income. In our modern era, legitimate opportunities with potential are abundant. The right ones can not only replace your income and fund your current lifestyle, but they can make you a whole new kind of rich. If you're the type of person who likes to have their cake and eat it, too, read on. I will guide you to do what others who are no smarter, more educated, or more connected than you have done.

Often, our beliefs hold us back from redefining our relationship with money in a way that helps us thrive. How many of these sound familiar?

"There's no such thing as a free lunch."

"If you don't work, you don't eat."

"Money doesn't grow on trees."

"This is the way the world works—just get a job."

We absorb these beliefs from our parents, society, educators, and peers. They sound reasonable, since most everyone we know, love, and admire lives by them. We buy into the paradigm and internalize it, never questioning if there is another way. Our life becomes about getting the big Ps: a pay increase, a promotion, or a pension rather than more choice, freedom, and fulfillment.

[4]

THE CURSE OF TIME BANKRUPTCY

BY DEFINITION, WEALTH IS "AN abundance of resources." Money is a resource, to be sure, but it is only one. The sad thing is that so many people give up so many other resources in an attempt to get wealthy (in terms of money). In the end, they may get the money they were after, but are bankrupt of every other resource that makes for a rich and fulfilling life.

Thomas Jefferson wrote in the Declaration of Independence that every person has a right to life, liberty, and the pursuit of happiness. Our country was founded on the principle that we have a right to be free and use that freedom to do what makes us happy. Those rights mention nothing about work or money.

 Entrepreneurs are willing to work 80 hours a week to avoid working 40 hours a week."

—LORI GREINER

But here's the thing. You gotta pay to play. You need money to buy freedom and pursue happiness. Unless you have very cheap tastes and no need for anything beyond food and shelter, it takes money to live well! So, by all means, money is necessary, but it is not all there is to living a rich life.

What if wealth was not only about having plenty of money but plenty of time? Youth? Energy? Health and vitality? Purpose and choice? If you want more of those *and* the Benjamins, read on.

Beyond just having a narrow definition of wealth, there's an even more insidious myth about money into which we can be indoctrinated. Let me tell you, I'm going to make some enemies on this one. It's the myth of entrepreneurship. We are led to believe that the ultimate dream is to "be our own boss." You are told to own your own business, be the CEO, be a boss babe. I was trapped in this paradigm myself for years.

Here's the stark reality: entrepreneurs are often less time rich than the nine-to-five crowd! To add insult to injury, the vast majority of entrepreneurs are also broke. Ouch. They are *wantrepreneurs*. If you ask them why they became an entrepreneur, they will tell you that they want freedom or they want to make a lot more money, but often they have little of either.

They would never admit it to themselves or to anyone else, but what they really own is not a business but a job. Granted, many entrepreneurs are extremely well paid compared to their W2 earning counterparts, but the data reveals most of them make only slightly more. While the nine-to-fiver puts in forty hours a week and then leaves for home, the entrepreneur puts in sixty or seventy hours a week and takes that work home at night.

As of 2021, the average entrepreneur makes $74,000 yearly, or $35.68 hourly. The bottom 10 percent make roughly $41,000 a year, while the top 10 percent make $134,000."

—ZIPPIA

You thought this was going to be a book about entrepreneurship? Not exactly. Put down your torches and pitchforks for just a moment. This is a book written for passivepreneurs. The idea here is not about who you work for. It's about how much you work. It poses an even more provocative and powerful question: *Why work?* So, yes, this book is for those who have someone else sign their checks as well *as* those who sign their own.

Mark Twain famously wrote, "Find a job you enjoy doing, and you will never have to work a day in your life." But I disagree with Twain. What if there's no job description for what you love to do? What if the thing you love to spend your time on doesn't pay a dime? For example, how many of us could realistically pay the bills playing golf? Exploring the globe? Can most parents make a living raising kids or being a painter? The point is not that you can't make money from some of these activities, but rather, why would that be a worthy goal? Pay is not ultimately what makes these activities worth pursuing. Pay is not the reason you love them in the first place.

So if jobs are not ideal (unless we do them for the sheer joy of it) and being our own boss is not necessarily the answer, what is? The answer is to identify a source of income that can meet your financial needs that is not dependent on you. A source that is not earned income or money that you trade your time for. A source that will allow you to spend your time doing what you want with no thought of what it pays or even if it pays.

 'Do what you love and the money will follow' is bull excrement."

—ME

Passive income and pursuing your passion do not need to be related. If you want to create passive income, choose the very best vehicle to get there. Don't take a passion and try to make it pay. Your passion does not need to be tied to making money and making money does not have to be sourced in anything at all that you love! Don't confuse the two. I got news for you: very, very few of the passions we want to pursue in life will support us and neither should they. Stop trying to do what you love in the hope that money will follow. Instead, make money follow you so you can do what you love for the rest of your life!

You are in no way guaranteed to make money with what you are passionate about. This is one the biggest lies we've been sold. For every Jay-Z and Lady Gaga in the world, there are five million musicians who are as in love with music, and maybe nearly as talented, but don't get paid a dime. For every Tiger Woods there are millions of golf lovers who would play till they drop every day but have no shot of ever turning pro. For every Elon Musk and Jeff Bezos, there are a gazillion burned-out wantrepreneurs who are broke and likely should have never begun working for themselves because they have zero passion for it.

The idea here is that our source of money does not need to be our source of happiness, fulfillment, and joy in life. Let me rephrase that: it is possible to list all the greatest joys of life without ever listing work as one of them! Bring out the pitchforks again!

Okay, this is where I need to add something. Based on multiple surveys, at least 50 percent of people do not like their jobs. A small percentage of the other 50 percent actually love their work. If you're in that small group, congrats! Go forth and enjoy your dream job. You, my friend, are blessed. This book is not for you. It's for the rest of us.

 We are human beings, not human doings."
—THE DALAI LAMA

Money is not like food where you get to enjoy various flavors and varieties. A dollar is a dollar is a dollar. It doesn't matter how it was earned; it all spends the same. So it makes no difference what business or vehicle you use to earn those dollars (assuming they are earned in an ethical and moral way). There is no more value in a dollar because you "earned" it than there is in one you did nothing to earn today.

My hope is that as we explore this new philosophy of money-time, you will be able to identify many new sources of income. These passive income vehicles (PIVs) don't need to be in your area of expertise and may even be down the road anyway. But before we start identifying potential PIVs and how we can start putting them to work for us, let's get a better understanding of why, contrary to what you've been told, time is not money.

 On a long enough time line, the survival rate for everyone drops to zero."

—CHUCK PALAHNIUK, *Fight Club*

LIFe
WORTH > NET
WORTH

[5]

YOUR NET WORTH IS NOT WORTH YOUR LIFE

WHETHER YOU'RE MAKING MINIMUM WAGE or you're an attorney or surgeon who makes hundreds of dollars an hour, we all put a price on our time. We have an amount that we are willing to accept in exchange for our time. We're so focused on this exchange and getting the most out of it as possible that we rarely ever stop to ask what our time is truly worth.

I live in Charleston, South Carolina, the most beautiful small city on Earth (scientific fact). One of my favorite places to visit here is St. Michael's Church in the downtown historic district. Behind that church is a graveyard that I frequent. Now, before you think I'm a psycho, graveyards in Charleston are not your average cemeteries. They are sublime, peaceful, and incredibly beautiful. In fact, they are so popular that roving groups of tourists pay guides to show them around. Visitors get to hear the long history of hidden cemeteries dotted around the historic churches.

I like to sit on my favorite stone bench next to St. Michael's and gaze at magnificent oak trees draped with Spanish moss. All around me are crumbling headstones from centuries past. It's like looking back into history. Many of these graves date back to the seventeeth century. Two signers of the American Constitution are buried there alongside long-forgotten commoners who once lived in the city.

On my last visit I noticed there are a few pieces of information on every headstone. There is a name, some words or a quote, and two numbers—year born and year deceased. No matter how worn the gravestone, whether it's from this year or two hundred years old, they all have one more thing: a dash between the two numbers. The dash represents an entire life from birth to death. That dash represents the decades, years, days, and minutes that the person buried below ground was given. That's how short our life is. It's a dash.

The reason life is so precious is that it is limited. It is finite. Life can't be multiplied, it can't be saved up, and it can't be stored away to be used in the future. I hate to be morbid, but when we get to that second date on the headstone, that's it. In a world of unlimited resources, wealth, and opportunity, time is so incredibly scarce. We can become more conscious of the time passing and no longer allow others to dictate how we spend it. We determine what matters, whether it's being with those we love, following our passions, or having the great experience of life. We must come to the realization that there is no dollar value we can place on that dash.

INCOME
+
TIME
+
CHOICE
=
TRUE
WEALTH

[6]

THE KEYS
TO CASH FLOW

OVER THE YEARS, I'VE MET some high-achieving, high-net-worth individuals from diverse industries, many of whom are superstars in their respective arenas. These achievers are obscenely financially wealthy. They have all the material wealth, the toys, the houses, even fame. I admired them. I wanted to be like them. Over time, I had the opportunity to get to know some of them personally.

What I learned, once I got to know some of them, is that their lives were not as they looked from the outside. They often had serious personal problems. Their marriages were falling apart or had already ended. Their kids didn't know them. They had many business associates, but few real deep relationships. Millions of followers but no friends. Outside of their rock-star career and material wealth, they had little to envy. And most notably, they all had a massive lack of time. Not all is what it seems in the land of the super successful.

Were they happy? Some who were open enough to answer that question off the record told me, "Hell no!" This situation is certainly not true of everyone who's super rich but was true often enough that it made me look closer at what was going on. These high achievers had paid the price and been willing to give everything to get the "wealth" they were after, but was it worth it? You'd have to ask them. I decided that, for me, wealth was only partially based on financial abundance and that it must not take first priority.

There are two money realities I believe most people find themselves stuck in. There is the reality of poverty and being forever in lack. A reality of needing money and never having enough of it and never experiencing financial breakthroughs. Many of us have been there or are there now. But there is an even more insidious reality most of us would hardly call a bad one: that of being wealthy.

 Be careful what you wish for, lest it come true."
                                        —AESOP

What if you did have the bank account balance with two or three commas and you owned all the shiny expensive toys and material prizes, but you had to exchange everything else you value for it? What if having it required you to give up the best years of your life in exchange? What if it meant each year, you'd work harder and longer than the year before? What if that type of wealth costs you your health? What if you had to pay with your youth? What if you reached the end of your life and wished not for more zeros in your bank account but more time with your now grown kids, a more fulfilling marriage, close meaningful friendships, or spiritual fulfillment? Here's the newsflash: every one of those also requires time, energy, and focus. If you think only money will comfort you, you'll miss out on the things that bring clarity and depth to your life.

So what am I preaching? Should you give up wanting more and go live in the mountains as a monk? If that's your thing, by all means go for it. But that's not what I'm pointing toward. What I'm saying is that, for many, money has become the goal in and of itself. It is a game in which the winner dies with the highest score.

> **I've never in all my years seen a hearse pulling a U-Haul."**
>
> **—GREG PAGE**

So what is the solution? Do we need to give up the idea of being rich? Are wealth and happiness mutually exclusive? Not at all. We just need a more complete definition of wealth. We need to make sure what we're aiming for is what we get. Because the secret is that you can have all the financial abundance you desire—as well as the time to enjoy it and the people to enjoy it with.

Investopedia defines wealth as "the accumulation of scarce resources." If that's true, let's talk about scarcity for a moment. How scarce is money? Well, if you have little, you may answer, "Very!" But money is infinite. There is no limit on the amount of wealth in the world. It used to be based on scarce resources such as gold and silver. But today it's not real. It's just digits in a computer. Wealth can be created from nothing. Instead of a zero-sum game, as some believe it is, you don't need to take a piece of someone's pie to get rich. You can bake your own pie. Wealth exists in unlimited quantities; it simply must be diverted into our lives.

Now let's take that definition of wealth—the accumulation of scarce resources—and apply it to time. Is time scarce? Well, if measured by the history of the cosmos, I would say not. But sadly, we do not live for billions of years. We have an expiration date that is infinitely shorter than the life of a galaxy. We have a dash. So time is extremely scarce. It's priceless!

Let's talk about the scarcity of elements found on Earth. Since iron is thousands of times more abundant than gold, an ounce of iron is worth about fifty-five cents, while the same amount of gold is worth $1,800. The value of gold versus the value of iron is roughly equivalent to the ratio at which each is found on the planet. That is how we determine the "price" for anything. It's either priced in terms of its scarcity, or it's priced according to what someone will pay for it (aka the free market).

How scarce are the resources we most value in life? How scarce are great people and relationships? How limited is your energy and focus? What would you pay to have another day back with someone you love who isn't here with us anymore? It's not only an interesting thought experiment, but a way of reordering what we value.

Of all the resources we can acquire to live the good life, money is in fact the most abundant, not the scarcest. But money is absolutely necessary because without it, we have no way to free our time, energy, focus, or our lives.

This viewpoint is not shared by many in our culture. Society values monetary wealth as an end in and of itself. It's not. Let's stop kidding ourselves. No one wants filthy papers with pictures of dead men on them. No one wants digits on a bank statement. What we want is what that money can buy us. But if we spend all our time, energy, and choices only trying to get the Benjamins, we may lose our life in the process. Money is the means, not the end. It is a tool, and a tool's only purpose is to be used for some greater purpose.

 For what purpose does it profit a man to gain the whole world and yet lose his soul?"

—MARK 8:36

I'd like to share my definition of wealth. Wealth is an abundance of passive income, discretionary time, and free choice. Breaking it down further, passive income is defined as cash flow that requires minimal labor to earn or maintain. Discretionary time is the hours available each day to spend as we see fit. Free choice is the amount of free agency we have to be, do, and have what we want in life. Here it is put simply:

PASSIVE INCOME

+

DISCRETIONARY TIME

+

FREE CHOICE

=

TRUE WEALTH

By expanding our definition of wealth, we can end up enjoying not just a large bank account but a rich life. After all, what's the point of creating financial abundance if it is ultimately tied to other people's plans for us? By having each of these three elements in abundance (passive income, discretionary time, and free choice), we truly have the ability to create an exceptional life for ourselves and the ones that we love.

[7]

BACK TO THE NEW FUTURE

WHEN YOU READ THE WORDS "get rich quick," what is your gut-level reaction? For most people, it's a very negative one. We are often warned not to fall for "get-rich-quick schemes." There are a lot of scams in the world, so it's no wonder so many are cautious.

But you know what else you should be wary of? Get rich *slow*. Be very, very careful with that one. If you believe that you can only get rich slowly, not only will you run the risk of not ever getting rich (you may die first), but if you do somehow become wealthy it will be a long, long time from now. I don't know about you, but I don't have thirty or forty years to wait and find out if I can fit a walker in my Lambo.

Not only am I going to go out on a limb again, but this time I'm bringing my own saw with me. Are you ready for it? "Get rich quick" is not a scheme! It's a limiting belief. A belief that will blind you to opportunities right in front of you. You can be right on this one or you can be rich, but you can't be both.

Here's the truth: every day, countless people are pulling themselves from broke and in debt to financially free. They go from zero to six, seven, and even eight figures in a few years. Many of them are doing it much quicker than that. Why? They do not have such a limiting belief. They are also in the right vehicle. I'll teach you more about vehicles in just a minute.

Be careful who you take your money advice from. From now on only take it from wealthy people. Better yet, take that financial advice only from people who've gotten that way quickly. They'll agree with me and tell you it can be done.

If you're on the traditional path to wealth, you may be doing work you aren't excited about. Perhaps you're saving what you can and investing it, with the hope to one day enjoy the fruits of your labor. But if when you finally get there you have one foot in the grave, you're in the wrong vehicle. The solution isn't looking for a *better* vehicle (more pay, better job, working harder), but to find a *new* vehicle. Think of this as like trading in the horse and buggy not for a faster or bigger buggy but for a fully self-driving Tesla. Or better yet, a Tesla mounted on a rocket that is now circling Mars (this actually happened!).

The shortcut to becoming a passivepreneur is simple. We must find vehicles that have worked consistently for others, and then get in those vehicles ourselves. We don't need to reinvent what works and we don't need to be pioneers; we can simply follow what's been proven to work. I'll share some niches I've discovered that are the best for generating passive (or semipassive income). I'll then show you the ways in which you can make them work for you.

We will also explore many opportunities in the online arena. The power of digital opportunities is that anyone can get into them. If you have an internet connection and a smart device, there are few barriers to entry. Not to mention, the digital world is where wealth is being created at the fastest pace in history. The point is, it now takes less and less time to create true wealth, but only if you're building that wealth in the right vehicle. The options are endless, and once you've shifted your perspective, you might discover even more.

When you learn which vehicle is a fit for you, I'll teach you how you can make sure you get the maximum income from the minimal time invested. You will learn how to focus your efforts only on those things that create passive income. You will then want to get to work building the machine that generates consistent cash flow. I'll also teach you methods that will keep you laser-focused when you do work. Working less is only accomplished through intense focus. I'll share some of my secrets to getting and staying focused. You'll learn it's a skill that can be developed over time, not something that you have to be born with.

In order to take this journey, we will first need to reevaluate our relationship with time, and forever cut the cord between time and money.

[8]

A SIMPLE CURE
FOR TIME SCARCITY

FROM THE TIME WE ARE young, most of us are taught that the ratio between time and money is one-to-one. You give up X amount of time in order to gain X amount of money. Then the game becomes about trying to increase the amount of dollars we get for each of those hours. We aim to make more per hour, a bigger salary, and so on.

The challenge with this line of thinking is the pesky fact that there are only twenty-four hours in a day. You can try to radically increase your dollars per hour, but you will always run into the limited number of hours you have available to trade. This limitation applies beyond hourly employees. Even the most skilled workers, like doctors and lawyers, are limited by the number of hours they can work and the amount they can charge (even if it's high).

Free yourself by learning how to make money *independently* of time, giving you both wealth and freedom. You no longer have to exchange your time for money. You can create passive streams of income that make you money while you sleep. This new way of looking at time and money is the foundation of what we will explore in this book. We will forever separate in your mind that money and time are fixed to each other.

This philosophy has guided me since I was very young. I've been "unemployable" for most of my adult life, building passive income stream after passive income stream, traveling the world, and spending tons of time doing what I choose. I've learned how to become a passive income generator time and time again, even in crises. I learned how to create, control, and own assets: from creating an eight-figure business online, to publishing and selling digital products, to purchasing real estate and companies that create cash flow, to passively investing in commercial real estate. And it's not just me. Every day, people like you are becoming passivepreneurs as well.

I didn't learn how to do all of this overnight. It took years of studying wealth creation and trial and error when it came to creating my own income streams. But ultimately, I was able to build a multimillion-dollar income based on different PIVs. It's allowed me to do the things I've always wanted to do: attend an acting conservatory, do mission work, go on monthlong road trips, and spend more quality time with my family and friends. I'm able to pursue my passions. I get to watch my young kids grow up and share many adventures with them. That freedom is the best feeling, better than any amount of money.

FOCUS ON THE EXPONENTIAL

[9]

THE REMARKABLE POWER OF THE EXPONENTIAL

BEFORE ENJOYING THIS NEW LIFESTYLE, I first had to adopt some shifts in perspective, and you'll need to do the same. I had ideas about what I needed to do, but further worked to solidify them into the rules by which I would live. The first, and most important rule, is something we've already touched on: divorcing time from money.

When you see how precious time is and come to value it *more than* money, you can occupy a headspace that allows you to understand how you can create more of both. You can work less, and yet achieve your goals much faster. Once I was finally able to reject the time-equals-money paradigm, I could see opportunities to create the life I'd always envisioned. These opportunities didn't have arbitrary caps like $25 an hour or $100,000 a year.

If you're willing to put in time and effort up front—and both may be considerable if working a full-time job—you'll eventually reach a point where you will be free. You can trade forty hours a week for just a few. You can trade the forty-year plan for the four-year retirement.

Remember, even highly paid people do not earn exponential income. If you're a bank president, you may have a high income, but you can't go out tomorrow and make ten times more per hour than you did today. Your income is linear and so is the time on which it's based. But you can go out tomorrow and make ten times more than you did today if your income is exponential. All you need to do is create, own, or control one or several passive income vehicles. In the coming chapters I'll teach you how to find the best PIVs.

The trick about exponential growth is that it often looks like nothing is happening for a while. For example, which of these would you rather have: $100,000 in cash right now, or one penny doubled every day for thirty days? Most of us would take the $100,000. It's a lot of money, we don't have to wait for it, and a penny doubling over and over wouldn't be much. Think of the $100,000 as a salary. It's a salary that many people aspire to.

But if you understand the power of exponential growth, you would choose to take the second option. You pick up that one red penny and work your ass off to double it the next day. Think of this second option as becoming a passivepreneur.

So what happens in this second scenario? A full week of effort and toil and struggle and you get paid sixty-four cents. Congrats! This is fun, right? But you decide to stick with it. By day eighteen that penny doubled is only $1,300. Crap. Three weeks of doing this damn thing and I get a lousy $1,300? I'm glad I didn't quit my day job.

You see, with exponential growth, we are easily tricked into believing that since very little has happened in the past, that very little must be in store for the future. So we throw in the towel. That's precisely what most people do. It might not happen at day eighteen; it may be six months in. Or a year. But they do eventually quit. So they opt in for taking the salary instead. They feel good knowing precisely what they will make this year.

But they have not chosen the path of wealth. They will never know that thirty days after choosing the penny, they would have $5.3 million and that in thirty-eight days it's grown to $1.3 billion! This, my friend, is exponential growth, and exponential is the playground of the rich.

Those who choose the exponential path often work for years while making very little. The only reason they are willing to do so is because they know they are playing in the right arena. It may look like they aren't succeeding, (remember that penny was only worth 64 cents after a week) but one day everything explodes upward. They look like overnight successes. You and I now know what really happened. They were smart enough to focus on building a source of income that has the potential to go exponential.

When I made my first money online, I earned in one night on a webinar nearly what I had earned the year before at my full-time job. Within weeks of making my first dollar online, I had brought in $178,393. By day 43, I had earned a cool million and earned a spot in the Two Comma Club. I also looked like an overnight success.

The truth was, I had invested a full year learning marketing, building out, writing, producing, and presenting an eight-week digital course. I created a ninety-minute webinar and a slide deck. I built out my sales funnel, and studied more than a dozen books on internet marketing. How much did I get paid during that year? *Zero*. Not one red cent. In fact I spent thousands during that year! I invested countless hours of my time, put my social life on hold, and made some real sacrifices.

How did I have the time? Because I was job-free. The first PIV that I set up was already supporting me financially and with very little input necessary from me. It was automated, cost me only a few hours a week to maintain, and was already making several hundred thousand dollars a year in profit when I started to create my second income vehicle. That was in 2017. Fast-forward to today and those PIVs still generate millions.

Most jobs don't have that power. Jobs are capped at whatever someone is willing to pay to fill that position. If you want to become wealthy, the only way to do it is with a vehicle that doesn't put any cap on what you can earn. The cool thing is you only need one of those to be a slam dunk.

The reason I made it when many others gave up had nothing to do with smarts. I wasn't successful because I had some kind of unfair advantage. What I did have in my corner was the unwavering belief in the power of the exponential. If you're spending your time building assets that have this potential and you have the patience to wait for it, the sky is truly the limit.

PART II
THE WAY

[10]

THE PATH TO PROSPERITY

I **'M NOT TYPICALLY A VIOLENT** person, but I do remember vividly the day that I murdered my alarm clock. I threw it against the wall with such force that it lodged itself halfway into the drywall. Now before you get all judgy, I didn't chuck it out of anger or in the middle of a fight in some kind of rage. I threw it with pure joy! The day I murdered my alarm clock was the day after I fired my boss.

I dreamt of that day for so long that when it finally arrived, I decided to celebrate. I decided I'd do that by sleeping till noon. So when that puppy went off at six-fifteen, I chucked it with glee. Back under the warm covers I remembered what a mentor of mine once said: "True freedom means never needing an alarm clock."

Before that day, the first thing that went through my body when I woke up was a sharp sense of dread. Dread that I was going to have to leave my warm cozy bed, hobble into the kitchen, and slurp down half a gallon of black coffee to get my brain jump-started. Dread that I'd have to rush to my car, where I would sit in traffic with a bunch of other poor souls who looked like they too would rather stay in bed.

I knew already how the day would play out because each day was pretty much like any other. I'd be forced to make small talk with coworkers that I couldn't care less about and quite frankly didn't even like as human beings. They'd complain about why life sucked, and I'd agree. A project or three would be dropped in my lap by lunchtime, and after the midafternoon slump I might take a micro nap between calls. In the afternoon I'd surf the web looking for ideas for my next vacation, which was five months away. Most destinations were the kind I could never afford to visit. Then I'd do it all over again the next week.

But that morning was different. It was like I was catching up on sleep for the last eight years of my life. When I finally rolled out of bed that afternoon I had a slight feeling of anxiety.

Wasn't I supposed to be doing something right now? Do I need to be somewhere? Should I be at work? Am I an idiot who just left a well-paying secure job with benefits and a 401(k) in order to sleep in every day? Am I a lazy bum?

I ran over to my computer and logged into my Airbnb account. I looked at the numbers and saw that on my four listings I had roughly $1,200 coming in that day—more than I took home all week at the job. I remembered my virtual team was on top of cleaning my listings and messaging guests. I hired them to make sure my little business kept humming without me. I sat there thinking how incredible my life had become and took a deep breath.

It didn't seem legal, what I was doing. I mean, who gets paid not to work? But I reminded myself that I *had* worked hard. So much time, effort, blood, sweat, and tears were invested into building this PIV so that one day it would not require much of my time to maintain.

Today, many years later, I've been able to help thousands of other people navigate this journey and kill their own alarm clock.

I've had them report back to me on the feeling they experienced on their day zero—the day they woke up and were 100 percent free.

It's an exciting place to be, but before we can get there, we need to talk about the practical roadmap. You're not going to wake up one day by accident and arrive. And contrary to what you may hear, it's not going to be easy for most of us. In fact, it may require us to work harder for a period of time and have less choice and less freedom until we get to the point where we can jettison the job.

SEEDS

FEED YOU FOR A DAY.

PLANTED SEEDS FEED YOU FOR LIFE.

[11]

THE BAKER
AND THE FARMER

BEFORE YOU CAN FIRE the boss, you'll need to keep your current source of income as is until you're ready to pivot (I'll tell you when to take the leap in a later chapter). First, you'll want to tighten your belt, so you have the money to fund your first PIV. The sooner you tighten that belt, the sooner you'll be in a position to be able to work less and have more. Here's how to cut the fat:

1. SAVE YOUR SEEDS

Seeds can be used for two main purposes: to be consumed or to be planted. Think about a bag of wheat seeds; you can pulverize them into flour and bake them into a nice bread, but once you carb out and eat that loaf, that's it—no more seeds. You get to enjoy those seeds, but only once.

> By definition, saving—for anything—requires us to not get things now so that we can get bigger ones later."
>
> **—JEAN CHATZKY**

What if instead, you used those seeds to plant an entire field? The next season you'd have enough wheat to make bread for the rest of your life! It's no surprise bread is slang for money, right?

So why do most of us eat our seeds? Because bread today sounds so much easier than being a farmer. Bread is warm and delicious and is right there ready to be slathered with butter and jam. Getting up at the crack of butt to fire up the tractor every day? Not so sexy.

A big challenge I see that keeps people from becoming wealthy is that they never get to the point where they have any excess capital to put at risk or invest. So you may need to get creative to find the money. For some, that may mean borrowing, but I believe that the best way is to use your own cash. I recommend saving at least 20 percent of your take-home pay for your startup fund.

Every year the Bureau of Labor Statistics breaks down the average budget for US households. I won't bore you with every category they report and what the numbers are for each. Instead, I'm going to lump a lot of things together for simplicity. By keeping all possible expenses to three categories, it allows us to see where the biggest chunks of underutilized cash can be found, cash that will fuel what we will build later.

Housing: 35 Percent of Budget

Let's tackle housing first. Roughly a third of our budget goes to keeping a roof over our heads. As the single largest expense in our life, it should be the very first place we look to carve out huge savings.

If you're single, bring on a roommate or two for a season. Consider taking a spare room and listing it on Airbnb for a few weekends a month; you could bring in a tidy sum. I was able to make enough doing this (before I built it into a full-on PIV) to cover my entire rent and utilities. I was an apartment hacker!

Do you own your home? Immediately look into refinancing. Not only could you reduce your payment, but you may be able to skip a month or two as those payments can be rolled into the new loan. While you're at it, now would also be a good time to shop around for a better rate on your homeowners policy. Total savings: 5–35 percent.

Recurring: 50 Percent of Budget

Recurring expenses are those that take place consistently and predictably and are essential for living. Recurring expenses take up half of all expenditures. They include car payments, gas, repairs, insurance, healthcare, food and meals, retirement contributions, debt payments, and more. These expenses are going to mostly be nondiscretionary—that is, you will need to pay them, so it's largely a matter of saving where you can.

How? You can eat at home exclusively. Try rice and beans or mix it up with beans and rice. Want serious motivation? Make your meals boring. Every meal you eat will remind you of the commitment you made to hit your goal. You'll have plenty of money and time later to go to the hottest restaurants and bars every weekend and pig out on your favorite foods. Skip going to Starbucks or picking up your favorite treat at the drive-through. Shop for better rates on every one of your insurance policies. If you haven't done this in a few years, you'll be shocked. Look around and you can find ways to cut the fat figuratively and literally. Total savings: 5–10 percent.

Discretionary: 15 Percent of Budget

Okay, this is where it gets fun. There is a lot of meat on the bone in this category. If you haven't already been able to carve out 20 percent on the first two, this is where you're going to make up serious ground. Think of discretionary expenses as the cracks your money seeps through after everything else is paid. When you ask yourself, "Where did all my money go?" this category is the answer. These expenses are usually compulsive, unconscious purchases that are generally the result of wants and not needs. Are you ready? This one may hurt a little . . .

Not-so-fun fact: the average person spends 3.1 hours a day watching TV and streaming services, according to *U.S. News & World Report*. Cut it all out. You don't need cable or Netflix. You will not die, I promise. Cancel anything else that is not essential: Pandora, Spotify, Audible, Stitch Fix, book club, hot sauce of the month club. Nothing is sacred. Stop spending money on entertainment, cocktails, splurging on new clothes, or dates. If you must absolutely have a love life, be a cheap date and take them to a park or animal shelter. You'll save a fortune.

Okay, I get it. This might all seem draconian, but every day that you choose to spend less is a day your brain will be triggered to take action. Every item you eliminate that you otherwise enjoy sends a signal to your subconscious that this is *not* the time to take it easy. This is *not* business as usual. This time it's going to be different. If you want radically different results you need to get radical. What else are you going to do now with all this free time and money other than go make your dreams happen?

Listen, I was right where you are now. I had to carve out that 20 percent so I had resources to get the tools, knowledge, and help I needed. I knew that if I was going to radically change my life, I would have to change my patterns and habits around how I spent money and time. The fascinating thing about tightening the belt financially and eliminating the nonessential is that it can lead to more freedom, not less!

2. RUTHLESSLY REDUCE

A lot of the expenses I cut in the early days fell into the category of "entertainment." I canceled my cable, cut the streaming services, and deleted the social media apps on my phone. I know. It sounds extreme, but it won't kill you to live like an eighteenth-century monk. You might even think better about yourself in the process, unplugging from the nonsense.

I mean, really, if you hadn't seen any of those binge-worthy shows, would your life be worse? You can ruthlessly reduce both your expenses and your distractions and increase the room you have in both your money and your time budget. You need food, shelter, and clothing; you do not need entertainment. Give it up for a while. That energy and time can be put to good use.

The best part of making this sacrifice is that every time you grab the remote control, you'll remember what you're up to. You'll remember that the time you'd otherwise throw away with mindless distractions can now be invested into building what will set you free. The more extreme you get with this, the faster you'll get there.

When I first set the goal of launching my second passive income source, selling digital courses, I didn't have a clue. But I did know the only thing that would ultimately stop me would be me either giving up or getting distracted. I usually fell for the second option. So I told myself, "I do not *deserve* TV or social media until I make a million dollars." It felt like my "burn the ships" moment. I took every minute I would have entertained myself and instead spent it to educate myself; essentially, I replaced distraction with discipline. Was it hard? Yes. Was it worth it? Absolutely.

Do you want extreme results in life? Get extreme! Get weird. Heck, I was single at the time, so I completely gave up dating for months. I was focused, my friend. I was truly feeling the sacrifices I was making and that gave me even more rocket fuel I could use to propel me toward success. You might not decide to give up the same things I did, but you *will* need to sacrifice. Decide today how to ruthlessly reduce anything that does not directly and immediately help you get closer to your goal.

3. FLOW THAT CASH

By now you've made some sacrifices, drastically cut back on your expenses, and have been able to set aside some money that will help you buy your freedom. The last step is especially important because you're going to now turn earned income into passive income. You're going to turn cash into cash flow. There are three paths you can take when investing your seed money to launch a PIV. You can do so by doing it yourself (DIY), by what I call Learning and Earning, or by following the leader. Let's take a closer look at each.

[12]

SAY GOODBYE TO DIY

THE FIRST AND MOST OBVIOUS way to use your seed money is by doing it yourself (DIY). The good thing about DIY is that it allows you to feel like you're 100 percent in control. You are, which is the best and worst thing about it. The problem is, you don't know if the actions you're taking are the ones that are going to get you the results that you're after. Since you're likely in a business or niche that you've never been in before, you're operating in the dark. Building a business by searching on Google may work for some, but it's not the most efficient way to operate.

Also, when you are doing it DIY style, you often don't know the best place to invest the 20 percent you've saved. For example, when I first tried to make money online, I went out and spent on the things that I thought I needed. I bought a domain, I signed up for some marketing software, and I went to the computer store and got a new laptop. I bought the tools that I believed would help me get started quickly. But almost none of that money directly contributed to moving me forward. I didn't need a new computer in the beginning. I signed up for unnecessary tools and I wasted my cash.

I was spending to build something I had little knowledge of, with no real strategy in place. Most of it was a complete waste of time and money. For every person who succeeds with the DIY method, there are ninety-nine others who run out of cash long before their business dreams become a reality.

LEARN AND EARN

You want to hear something that will piss you off? If you get a college degree today, your chance of finding a job quickly after graduating is about the same as winning a coin toss. The data shows that nearly half of college grads are still looking for work a year later[1] with many graduates searching years before landing their first post-degree job.

For those who do find work, only one in four will find a job that's in any way related to the major they chose,[2] and a full 40 percent of them will land a job that doesn't even require a degree in the first place![3] That's insane.

Let's also consider the true monetary cost of getting a degree. For those who live on campus and in state, the total expense for college tops $101,948 over four years. For those out of state, it's even more, coming in at $212,868 for four years. Once interest on student loans and the lost income from not working for four years is figured in, the true cost of a bachelor's degree may top $400,000!

Sadly, most college grads fail to demand a return on the substantial investment they've made in themselves. The higher education industry also distracts us from these facts by putting the true "value" of an education on the experience itself. The result is a nearly $2 trillion pile of debt riding on the shoulders of a new indebted class, many of whom will never be able to repay what they owe.[4]

What the business of higher education sells us (and it is a for-profit business, people) is a dream. The dream is this: spend four-plus years of your life and hundreds of thousands of dollars and you'll at the very least get a job in the field that you studied and, more importantly, land a job that you couldn't have gotten on your own! For some, the dream works out; but sadly for way too many, it does not. To add insult to injury, most college students don't even earn money during those four years. They are too busy studying to earn a diploma that many of them will find useless. Before you go hating on me, please hear that I am myself a college graduate. My degree is BS. I mean, it's a BS degree. I digress.

Imagine if you could spend considerably less time and money on an education and at the same time earn money while getting that education. Instead of spending four-plus years before you can determine if your investment was worth it, you can see results in a matter of months or even days. That's what learning and earning is all about. It means that you decide to use an education that is built on the framework of earning as you go.

A great example of this is network marketing. Many companies have comprehensive training and education not only for how to build the business but on a personal development level as well. I credit a lot of my personal growth to my involvement in network marketing when I was in high school. If you find a great company and put in the work, you can start making money quickly and at times substantial passive income. Yes, you can learn and at the same time earn.

I'll give you another example. I have a coaching program that helps my high-level students launch and scale an Airbnb business without owning properties. If students follow the program as I outline it, they are generally making money in the first sixty days or less. Not only are many making money in a month or two, but they are profitable as well. They can get a near immediate return on their investment and learn immensely valuable skills in the process.

The cost of my program is not cheap unless you compare it to the cost of a four-year degree. The average earnings at the end of the first year for those who complete our BNB Formula coaching program blow away the average salary college grads take home. In fact, some of my students are earning sums that would make Ivy League graduates blush.

The learn-and-earn model is a great way to self-fund your education while at the same time building passive income. It's much faster than the DIY path because you're following a proven, step-by-step model. The ultimate win-win game is to get paid to gain new skills.

FOLLOW THE LEADER

The final way to invest your seed money is the ultimate shortcut. It's more powerful than going out on your own or even learning and earning. This shortcut, "Follow the Leader," involves working with somebody who can lead you to the end result. This leader could be a coach, a mentor, or a teacher. The key to Follow the Leader is to identify someone who has already achieved the specific result that you're after and is now willing to teach you how to do the same.

The first time I thought about teaching what I knew online was about a year after I launched my Airbnb business. The idea to create my first course came about by accident. I had made over $300,000 my first year in the business and was working about three to four hours a week to run the entire thing. I was getting so many requests from friends, and friends of friends, to teach them what I was doing that I figured if I had a course available many of them would buy it. So I skipped over the DIY method and decided to learn and earn.

I absorbed as much information as I could about online marketing and applied what I was learning, and I did build out an amazing course—but I hit a wall. I tried to sell it online and nobody wanted it! I was dumbfounded because I had held nothing back about my success with Airbnb in this program and I knew it would work for people. I was at an impasse. I put so much time, money, and effort to get to this point, only to see it flop.

Thankfully, I remembered something I had learned years before as a real estate investor. Any time you face an unsolvable problem, the answer to that problem can always be found by asking "who?" Not "what?" Not "how?" The first question should always be: *Who has done this before?*

For any challenge that we have in business, there's always someone out there who would have the ability to offer a solution based on their extensive experience. They see things from the eyes of experience and wisdom; our mountain is their molehill. I knew I needed somebody who could give me the insight I was missing. So I set out to find who that person was.

Later that week I saw a Facebook ad for a book called *Dotcom Secrets* by Russell Brunson. I bought the book, devoured it in one night, and then signed up to go to Russell's annual event called Funnel Hacking Live. It is still the premier global meetup for top internet marketers. It was a place where they could gather to learn, network, and share what they know.

When I arrived, I talked to as many people as I could. Many of them were making millions and even tens of millions of dollars per year online. I shared the idea for my course with as many of them as possible and they were all very positive about it. I asked for advice, but none of them really gave me the breakthrough that I needed.

On the last day of the event I met a guy named Akbar. He was there to receive an award. The Two Comma Club award was for someone who generated a million dollars in online revenue. He listened intently as I sold him on the idea I had for my course. I detailed all the challenges I was facing in getting it to sell, and I asked him if he could point me in the right direction. He told me, "I think I know how to fix your problem. Once you do, I truly believe you're going to go home and make millions of dollars."

I almost kissed him on the freaking lips right there in the ballroom. This guy believed in what I was doing! I had wracked my brain for months to figure out what I was doing wrong, and he knew what it was! Wow. I knew I had to work with this guy. "What would it take for you to work with me one-on-one to help me get to that next level?" I asked.

"Ten grand, up front," he replied matter-of-factly.

Unfortunately, that was more than what I had available at the time. So I answered with, "I'll give you $5,000 today and I promise to immediately put in place whatever you tell me to do." After considering my offer, he shook my hand and said he'd call me.

Three days later I was on our first phone call. He showed me what I was doing wrong with my sales page and how to correct it. It was like I was a stick figure living in two dimensions and he lived in the 3D world where he could see the whole picture. I was trying to keep up as he laid out what I needed to fix. He gave me so many next steps to take that, for the next thirty days, all I did was try to implement what he was teaching me.

Then another leader crossed my path. A marketer I didn't know named Steven Snyder reached out to me via email. He had seen one of my earliest failed attempts at running an ad on Facebook. He told me I had a great idea, but my approach was wrong. He offered to help me as well, if I agreed to do my first presentation for his email list.

A month and many calls with Steven later, I hosted my first webinar. I sold my course live to a group of people who had never heard of me. I had no following on social media, had never done a live presentation before, and had no endorsements. I was just a dude with a webinar about Airbnb and a guy named Steve who gave me a shot.

That night, after the presentation was over, I logged into Stripe, the merchant service I used to collect credit card payments. I was hoping to see $5,000 to recoup what I paid Akbar, or maybe even $10,000. The number that was in front of me was $64,342.93. *What?* That was nearly my annual salary at the job I walked away from a year earlier. I got on a call with Steve. He told me that a third of everyone who was on my webinar purchased the course.

The only reason I went from no sales to over $64,000 in one night was because I was following the leaders. I implemented what I was told to do by those who had done it themselves. Both Akbar and Steve gave me the breakthrough that I needed. They were so much further up the trail in the journey that, for both of them, showing me where I was stuck was simple.

In my mind, Follow the Leader is simply the very best investment one can make. It allows you to avoid many of the pitfalls and setbacks that otherwise are inevitable for the inexperienced. Life is short and Following the Leader is the best way to save as much of it as you can on the way to your destination. Remember, it's the first pioneers that take all the arrows and the second wave that gets to settle on the land.

The cool thing is, once you get to a certain point, you may end up being the leader and having people follow you! I'm humbled now that people seek me out. But no matter how successful I become, I never forget that there's always someone I, too, can follow.

[13]

HOME REMEDIES FOR "SHINY OBJECT SYNDROME"

WHEN I WAS ABLE TO automate my entire Airbnb business and no longer manage it myself, I shifted to helping and teaching people. I had freed up my time and could add on to my next vehicle. When that second vehicle was successful and on autopilot, I identified another PIV, which was coaching. Repeating the process, I launched into commercial real estate syndication, book publishing, software, digital products, affiliate marketing, and more. Each and every one of these PIVs continue to fuel my time-rich, option-rich lifestyle.

What is the first step to accomplish this for yourself? *Decide what you want.* Get clear on precisely what you want to achieve, and by what date. Who, what, where, how, and by when? Get it on paper, on purpose, and with a deadline. Instead of chasing after the latest shiny object, start with the end in mind. Napoleon Hill, author of *Think and Grow Rich*, puts it this way:

"Whatever the mind of man can conceive and believe, it can achieve. Thoughts are things! And powerful things at that, when mixed with definiteness of purpose, and burning desire, can be translated into riches."

Here's an example of someone with no definite outcome: "I want to be rich one day and be able to buy my dream house." The problem with that dream is that there's no way to measure whether or not they've achieved it. What kind of house? Is it owning a 30,000-square-foot estate in the Hamptons or a 400-square-foot tiny house? How do you define rich? Is rich paying your bills every month with enough left over to order whatever you want at Chili's on Fridays? Is rich sitting on a solid gold toilet inside your G6, which you just landed on the deck of your superyacht? Be as clear as possible when choosing your definite outcome.

The problem with not being specific is that your brain has no clear instructions on how to take the next step. Your mind has no measurable way to know if the moves you're making are getting you closer to your goal. By not articulating what success looks like, in detail, you can't possibly put together a roadmap that will get you there.

Here's a great example of articulating what you want:

"I will make $1 million per month after taxes every single month by January 1, 2024. I will do this by purchasing 1,000 B Class apartment units in the Southwest using none of my own money and by working directly under Bob McMoney."

Why is this statement so much more powerful? Because every month and every year that you get closer to January 1, 2024, you can see whether or not you are on track to achieve your goal. If you get to the end of next year and you have zero revenue and zero apartment units, you know you might not be on track.

If, however, you've purchased ten units and bring in $5,000 a month—even though that achievement may be just a drop in the goal bucket—you know you are making progress. Every step you take to add more units and generate a specific amount of income makes your goal, essentially, inevitable. If you keep doing the same action over and over again, you *will* hit your target of 1,000 units.

Will you achieve your goal by the time frame you've set for yourself? Maybe not. But ultimately, that's not what's most important. What's most important is that you now have a specific action plan that's measurable and has a deadline. Until you get specific about what you want, you're very unlikely to take any meaningful action toward achieving it. It's difficult to meet a friend at Starbucks unless you know what time they'll be there and *which* Starbucks. (There's one of those suckers on every corner.) You need both the destination and the time of arrival with any journey.

It's important to keep in mind that the timeline is going to be different for each step, and results might happen more quickly or slowly than you planned. Airbnb quickly generated cash flow in a matter of days, which gave me confidence early about that model, but the course took a year before I made a single dollar. Some PIVs I'm working on right now will likely take even longer, but the payoff will be magnitudes larger than any PIVs I have now.

But there's a warning here: if you are presented with a "business opportunity," the person you should ask about the business model's legitimacy is *never* the seller. You need to independently verify whether the model works. That means asking other sources, preferably those who have been through the same process or program.

For example, when I set out to become an internet millionaire, I saw a lot of products selling that dream. But it wasn't until I went to a big conference and sat next to dozens of people who were all making seven to eight figures online that I truly bought into that model as possible for me. I got my information and advice from people who had already produced the result I was after. These people had nothing at all to gain from me joining the program or buying the coaching I was offered. I was getting the real scoop, not being sold a dream. So I doubled down on the products and training offered with ClickFunnels at that event, and the rest is, as they say, history.

Ultimately, strategy eats opportunity for breakfast. You need to first think of where you want to be, develop a strategy to get there, and then and only then choose opportunities that fit your strategy. When starting with the end in mind, ask yourself, "If I were successful with this, what would that look like?" Be very specific. For example, "I want to be earning $10,000 a month spending less than five hours a month in this venture by October 5."

Once you decide to put all of your effort into that vehicle, don't look at anything else. Don't day trade and also try to be a vlogger. Similarly, don't jump into house flipping and also dabble in network marketing. Just pick one! Go out of your way to avoid "shiny object syndrome." No other factor has turned more entrepreneurs into wantrepreneurs. When opportunities present themselves, say *yes* only to those that pay you very well for your time (or will down the road) and *no* to everything else. Remember, there's an infinite number of opportunities, but there's only one life in which to pursue them.

WHO'S
DOWN WITH PIVs?

[14]

FOUR STEPS TO BECOMING A PASSIVEPRENEUR

NOW THAT YOU'VE GOT THE right understanding and mind-set, you need to focus on the four steps to firing your boss—forever. You will never go back to a life of being someone's employee. You are now unemployable. This is the path you will follow (and I will teach you).

STEP 1:
CALCULATE YOUR WALK-AWAY NUMBER

Let's first figure out your walk-away number (WAN). It's the amount of money you'll need to reach passivepreneur status. Let's start with what you take home after taxes and other deductions. I'm referring to the actual dollar figure that gets deposited in your bank account each month. Multiply that number by 1.5. This is your walk-away number.

Why 1.5? Because in order for you to make the leap, you'll want to have a cushion. This leap will account for any fluctuations in the PIV you'll be building, but it will also give you a psychological cushion. When you jettison the job, you need to know with confidence that it's the smart move. Worrying if you'll have enough once you go out on your own is the fastest way to create additional anxiety. So first give yourself a 50 percent raise. Then, and only then, put in your two-week notice. Let me give you a concrete example. On the last job I will ever have, I was taking home $5,765 a month. If you take that and multiply by 1.5, you get $8,674.50, or my WAN.

STEP 2:
SELECT YOUR VEHICLE

A PIV is an asset you own, create, or control that generates semi-passive or fully passive income. There are more PIVs than you can imagine, and you'll learn about many of them in this book. The important thing to remember is to choose one. Not two; not half a dozen; not a different one every few months. One. Decide and double down. It's essential to your success.

Your first PIV should be one that you can work at part-time outside of your job. Focus on the ones with the potential to hit your WAN in six to twelve months. Later in the book, you'll also choose to become first a creator, controller, or owner of assets and you'll learn many options for PIVs suited to each type of passive-preneur. In the coming chapters, we're going to talk about options like affiliate marketing, rental arbitrage, digital products, online coaching, and peer-to-peer lending.

STEP 3: SCALE THE PIV
UNTIL YOU REACH YOUR WAN

Scaling is increasing the income from your passive income vehicle while also decreasing the personal time required to maintain it. This is where the rubber meets the road. A warning here: it is vitally important that you choose a PIV that can be scaled in both directions. Over time, it can be scaled up on the income, and can also be scaled down on the personal hours required. Very few cool-sounding business ideas you run across will be scalable both ways.

Let me give you an example of a PIV we would not choose. You take your life savings of $50,000, buy a rental property, and rent it out long term. Now I love real estate investing and yes, it qualifies as passive income. But if that $50,000 you put down as a deposit is all the money you have, and that rental property only nets you $300 a month, you hit a wall. It may take you little to no time to manage that property, but it isn't scalable on the income side. It may be a great investment, but it does not qualify as a PIV.

Another example would be buying a franchise where you're the operator. Most franchises have the potential to scale on the income side, but if you don't have enough revenue to install someone as the operator, you can't scale down your hours. A perfect example would be a friend of mine who years ago bought a Subway franchise. He dreamed of being a jetsetter but spent years slapping cold cuts on Italian bread because he didn't remove himself from running the store. Don't be a Subway schlub.

Remember, we aren't looking for a second job, or even to be our own boss—we're looking for passive income! Your PIV must be a vehicle that allows you to quickly scale your income into the stratosphere and then eventually scale down your time involved. Choose wisely.

What happens once you hit your WAN? You are free, my friend! You're now officially a passivepreneur, and life is about to open for you in ways you never imagined. You are financially independent, and your financial destiny is in your own hands. Are you ready to become wealthy? Good. Move on to Step 4.

STEP 4:
STACK ADDITIONAL PIVS TO BUILD WEALTH

This is where things get spicy. At this point you've built a passive income source that requires less and less of your time. You've likely walked away from your job, and you have more choice, more money, and more time. Maybe you've even taken an offensively long vacation. Good for you. When you've had enough piña coladas and you're ready to get back at it, it's time to stack.

Passive Income Stack means to own, create, or control additional passive income vehicles beyond the first one. Doing so will allow you to create redundant, excess sources of income, and build long-term wealth. It isn't wise to be reliant on only one source at this stage. You can also use the additional income above and beyond your lifestyle requirements to reinvest in even more PIVs.

For me, once I had my first PIV humming along nicely (Airbnbs), I went from working "full-time" on the operation to spending only a few hours a week to oversee my small virtual team. I decided to take a sixteen-country, two-month world tour of all the places I'd always dreamt of seeing. I circled every place on a map I'd always wanted to go, bought a round-the-world ticket, and took off for the unknown. I was living my dream.

But while I was away, I got flooded with a bunch of questions on my social media posts and in my DMs:

"Are you a trust fund kid?"

"Don't you have a job you need to get back to?"

"How can you afford to do all the things you're doing?"

"Can you take me with you?"

"Is Kathmandu as weird as they say?" (Yes.)

With all these messages pouring in, suddenly my next PIV was staring me in the face. I had information people wanted! What if they would pay me to learn how to do what I did with my first PIV? So I flew home and got to work creating my next one.

You already heard about my online course and the webinar I created to sell it, but I left this part out: I kept perfecting that presentation over and over, and eventually recorded an "evergreen" version that would play on autopilot twenty-four hours a day, 365 days a year. People would land on my web page, give me their email address, and watch a ninety-minute presentation. At the end of it they could buy my $997 course—and bang, it went into my bank account. Other than updating the content as needed twice a year, I fully removed myself from working on that PIV.

Five years later, that one product has done tens of millions in sales, and it still generates income every week. PIV #2 in the can; I had stacked it on top of my already automated Airbnb business, and I was ready to keep stacking. I created digital tools, memberships, training, and produced a reality show called *House Hackers*. I also created a mini book that has now sold over 130,000 copies, generating seven figures. I launched a dozen other PIVs that all generate their own streams of passive income.

Even now, as you hold this book in your hand or listen to it on audio, the minute you purchased it, a small royalty went into my account. If you look closely there are even more PIVs sprinkled throughout this book. Imagine PIVs inside of PIVs. As Jim Carrey in *The Mask* would say, "Somebody stop me!"

Keep in mind, in less than a year I walked away from a six-figure job. Two years later, I made a million dollars. Three years later, I made multiple eight figures, and in less than two years will hit nine. That's what I call the short road to wealth! All those PIVs continue to work for me with minimal (if any) involvement on my part—and there's no reason you can't do the same. In a world of side hustles, stop working so hard and instead get stacking!

Four Steps to Passivepreneur Status
- Step 1: State your Walk-Away Number.
- Step 2: Select your first passive income vehicle.
- Step 3: Scale the PIV until you reach your WAN.
- Step 4: Stack additional PIVs (passive income stacking).

Need help finding your first PIV or the next one to add to your stack? I got you covered. Check out www.dontstartasidehustle .com/resources for the ultimate list, or scan below with your smartphone.

1. WAN -

- Walk Away # $1072.00 × 1.5 = $1,608
- 1st PIV - Online Store - Ekwid
- Scale the PIV until You Reach Your WAN
- Repeat - by Stacking another PIV.

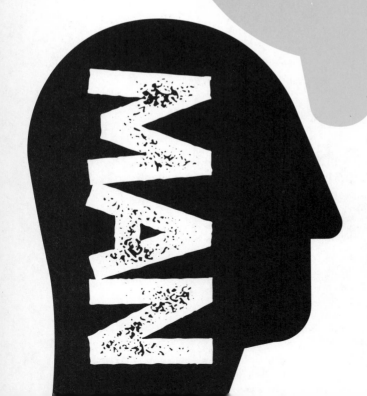

[15]

THE JOY OF SAYING NO

I N THE COMEDY FILM *Yes Man*, Jim Carrey's character, Carl Allen, is stuck in a boring life of mindless routines where he never takes any chances. One day Carl runs into self-help guru Terrence Bundley and has a life-changing intervention. Bundley shows him how to embrace the philosophy of saying yes to everything that comes his way. This one shift radically changes Carl's life. After saying yes to every crazy experience he finds himself in, he gets promoted at work, transforms into a confident version of himself, and even falls in love. What he learns is that the power of yes can change his life.

But this philosophy has major drawbacks, as Carl soon learns. Although Carl was a fictional character, many people in real life think just like him. They see every possibility and are so excited about every one of them that they never succeed at any of them! As you enjoy more success and income in your life, you also get to enjoy an abundance of opportunities. This sounds great, right? Wrong. More options are precisely what is most likely to take us off the path we're currently on.

Entrepreneurs tend to lean toward saying yes. They go down rabbit hole after rabbit hole, chasing the next great idea. But there's a better way. By making a solid commitment to reaching a goal, that goal becomes much more likely to be achieved.

Today, we have more choices than ever before in history, and while having choices is good, having *too many* can mean our attention is constantly being pulled in many directions by competing opportunities. Once you've chosen your vehicle, commit to it and say no to everything else until that PIV is humming along nicely.

The most important skill you can hone on your quest to become a passivepreneur is learning how to fully commit. Give yourself a time frame (for example, one to three years) during which you'll give it your entire energy and focus, until you see results. Don't give up before you hit exponential wealth. Remember we are not on a linear path, which means you may have to hang in there a bit longer to hit that exponential rise, and eventually achieve success.

Let's take a metaphor from the romantic world. Saying yes is sleeping around. Saying no is getting married. When you get married you promise to say no to everyone else—forever. But with that choice you may also find the fulfillment singlehood can't provide.

I'm married now, but for many years I thought "Till death do you part" was terrifying. Saying yes in this case is scary. What if I choose wrong? What if it doesn't work out? *I think I'll just stay single for life*, I reasoned.

This is how many of us approach business. We're promiscuous but want to enjoy the benefits of long-term commitment. We want to be able to walk away when things get tough rather than stick to it and put in the work. If we don't commit, we must settle for the results of our unwillingness to do so.

I'd rather say no to something that could have been great and succeed wildly at what I've committed to than say yes to small opportunities and never hit a grand slam. Even Babe Ruth, among the greatest hitters in the history of baseball, could only hit one ball at a time.

 When you say no to most things, you leave room in your life to really throw yourself completely into that rare thing that makes you say, 'HELL YEAH!'"

—DEREK SIVERS

ARE YOU A FLASH LIGHT

OR A LASER?

[16]

LASER-LIKE FOCUS FOR THE CHRONICALLY DISTRACTED

EARLIER IN THIS BOOK I included Lori Greiner's quote about an entrepreneur being someone who will work eighty hours a week for themselves to avoid working forty hours a week for someone else. Funny, but often painfully true. The pitfall for most entrepreneurs is that they accept the idea that they need to "hustle" and "grind" every day to succeed. It's become a badge of honor.

Here's the stark reality: hard work will be required to be successful in almost any field, but focused work is orders of magnitude more powerful. The ability to focus intently on a specific outcome for a few hours each day is what separates the winners from the winners who take all. Stop working so hard and instead work focused.

What if we shifted our priority from how many hours we work on our PIV to how much focused work is done in just a few hours? The ability to execute on your big objectives and ultimately make your dreams come true is directly tied to developing this skill. Read that sentence again and think about it, without distractions or moving on. Good work, my distracted friend!

It's ironic that I am the person teaching about focus. For the majority of my adult life, I've struggled with ADD. My best friend, Todd, even calls me "squirrel boy" because I have the gift of dropping whatever I'm doing at any moment at the slightest distraction. I'm like Dug the golden retriever in the movie *Up*, panting and eager but unaware of my unawareness. So trust me, if what I teach you here in this chapter has worked for me, it will work for you.

What I'm about to teach you about focus has nothing to do with your natural ability, temperament, or personality. Your level of focus is not based on your intelligence, nor is it a gift only a select few are born with. Focus is something you have; it is something you do. It is a skill (thankfully) that anyone can learn and develop. Think of focus as a mental muscle: the more time you spend exercising that muscle, the stronger it will become.

STEP 1:
CHOOSE *WHAT* TO FOCUS ON

We are often tempted to jump in and start ticking things off the to-do list so we can have a sense of accomplishment at the end of the day. But winning at life and business is not based on how many things we've checked off each week. You win by being crystal clear about the few big things you want to accomplish and doing <u>only</u> what moves you closer to each of those end results. By choosing a handful of big objectives to focus on, you will have a filter with which to say no to everything else. Here's the big takeaway: there is little value in focusing on the wrong things.

Focused work eats hard work for breakfast."

—**ME**

Your best hours each day are no longer going to be spent jumping around from activity to activity checking things off that don't matter. Your best time is now going to be spent only on what you decided in advance is most important. The clearer you can be on what you want to accomplish long term and the more willing you are to say no to everything else, the more focus you will enjoy.

Here's a powerful question to ask every morning: "If I work on only *one* project today that gets me closer to my ultimate outcome, what would that be?" Once you've identified that project, ask yourself, "What are the most important tasks that I would need to do today to make massive progress toward completing that project?" Those are the only tasks you will allow yourself to do today, during your focused block of time. Every other to-do item that comes outside of that list will have to wait.

STEP 2:
CHOOSE *WHEN* TO FOCUS

If focus is like a muscle that can be developed and strengthened, the same is true of willpower. We don't have willpower in unlimited quantities, nor is it constant throughout the day. Research has proven that each day we wake with a certain balance of available mental and physical energy. Throughout the day we draw from that balance until the point at which it nears zero. The same way you can work a muscle to fatigue, you can work your willpower to failure, and often long before you've gotten through your full day.

We've all been there. Here's an example: You put off doing your most important task all morning. Lunchtime arrives and you decide to grab a bite at the Mexican restaurant with Jim. You settle on a football-size burrito, chips, salsa, and a gallon of Diet Coke. Rolling back into the office ninety minutes later, you sit at your desk full and so done. The next few hours go by in a dragging blur until you finally close the computer and head home. You have a vague sense of *What the heck did I do today?* running around in your mind. It's not you. Often, we don't complete what we want to do each day because our willpower is at zero.

So what's the solution? Choose a block of time you will spend every day in a state of uninterrupted focus. Make it a top priority every single day. For some folks, that may be first thing in the morning. These people make me sick. I mean, what are you so cheery about that early? They wake up ready to go, happy about life, and firing on all cylinders. For others it may be late at night. Now, these are my people! The later it gets, the more energy they have. Regardless of what kind of person you are, the key is to decide in advance when you're going to block out focused time on your calendar. During this block of time, nothing else should be done.

When you're starting out, it may be difficult to do more than one or two hours of concentrated focus. But as you exercise this habit more consistently, you'll likely find you want to carve out more and more time for it. It's highly rewarding when you see the long-term results. For me, three to four hours a day, Monday through Thursday, works well. I save Fridays for catching up on all the "do later" tasks.

STEP 3:
CHOOSE *WHERE* TO FOCUS

You can have the concentration of a grand master chess player or the drive of Elon Musk, but if you choose to skip this third step, you will have a real challenge focusing effectively. Here's the key: the conditions under which you choose to complete focused work are more important than any other factor.

Studies have shown that brains do not work effectively if they are multitasking. Each time attention is even briefly interrupted by an external or internal input, or shifted to a new task, it takes roughly ten to twenty minutes to get back to the same deep level of focus from which you left. What this means is that every text message, every email, every coworker stopping by to say hello, or a quick glance at social media flushes a good quarter hour down the toilet.

Forget the trite advice of turning off notifications on your phone—put that sucker in airplane mode. Better yet, leave it in the car. It's hard to check your phone if it's not in the building. Getting extreme is what I'm talking about. But what about emergencies? Unless you run a 911 dispatch center, nothing is an emergency that can't wait for a couple hours.

"But, Brian, what if I need to be reached?" Before I got married I would've thought this was a ridiculous question. Now I have a wife and two kids and the idea that they can't get a hold of me at all times doesn't fly. After all, what if an emergency comes up with one of my kids or my wife needs to speak with me about something urgent? I needed to find a way to become almost always unreachable, except in certain circumstances. I found a simple fix: I got a bat phone.

Just like Batman had a special hotline that the city could call when they needed him to squash a crime spree, I also have a bat phone in my office. It's a good old-fashioned, hardwired phone, although it could just as easily be a cell phone. The only person who has that number is my wife. I can relax, knowing that when my cell phone is off, I'm still accessible to those who are most important.

The point here is to be creative. Come up with your own solution, but make sure it's one that protects the time you've committed to spend each day in focused work.

If that block of time does not involve a computer screen, this would be a great time to put all of those black mirrors in the other room. Grab a pen and paper or even just sit and think if that's what you most need to accomplish. If you do need to be on the computer, close out every application and browser except the one that you need for the next few hours. Do not under any circumstances open that email account. It's a ticking time bomb of distraction. Essentially, you are cutting off from the outside world for a bit. Don't fall for the idea that you won't be tempted because you turned off everything. You will want to send out a quick email or shoot a text to somebody as it may relate to what you're doing. The minute you take that pill, you're sucked right back into the world of reaction. It's also important that, before you start this block of time, you first collect all the tools you'll need. Think through if you have everything you need in advance.

A focused environment is more than eliminating notifications. You can have all those things turned off, but if you're sitting in a busy Starbucks with music playing and strangers walking by, and the espresso machine making that awful sucking sound, that, too, can be a less-than-ideal environment in which to focus. If you need to work near others, I recommend using noise canceling headphones, playing white noise or music, and facing in a direction that allows no one to pass through your field of vision.

Don't panic. We're talking about a block of time, not the entire day. I know this all may sound strict to you, and that's because it is! The stricter you are with these blocks, the more freedom you get to enjoy. Imagine going into work and three or four hours later you can leave (if you work for yourself now or in the near future).

It's possible, because not only did you accomplish more in those hours than you would normally accomplish in a few days, but you also only worked on your most important objective. If, at the end of the day, you've done only what truly matters and you've done as much of it as you could in that block of time, what else really matters?

How do you know if you followed the three steps effectively? You'll know because when your timer goes off at the end of the block, the time will have flown by. You will have entered a flow state where you're so absorbed in what you're doing that you're no longer even aware of time. This state is not only a great way to make exceptional progress, but it's also a rewarding and ultimately fulfilling way to live!

Wrapping up, there is one caveat that I must make regarding the effectiveness of mastering focus. None of the three prior steps have any value if you don't create a new habit. Consistency is the glue that holds it all together and will give this newfound skill immense compounding power over time. It isn't enough that you do this once or periodically—it must become who you are. Once you have ingrained this habit into your daily habits, you'll be astounded at what you can do.

PART III

THE WEALTH

MODELING
OVER
MASTERY

[17]

MODELING FOR AVERAGE-LOOKING PEOPLE

RESEARCH HAS SHOWN THAT IT takes roughly 10,000 hours to fully master a skill. This is true whether you aim to be an expert-level violin player, do a triple axel as an ice skater, or become a blockbuster movie producer. Mastery is a path to success, but only if doing that skill is how you want to spend your 10,000 hours. Do it for the love of the thing you are mastering. But there is another less time intensive way to get extraordinary results and that is the path of modeling.

Modeling is not about mastering a particular arena yourself, but hiring a master to help you get the same result. I don't have to spend thousands of hours testing, refining, experimenting, failing, reinventing, and practicing. I can talk to the guy who already did it. He may allow me to cut that 10,000 hours to 100. I may not become a master myself, but I can get most of the results of one. Since we want to be on the short path to wealth, we simply don't have 10,000 hours to give. We don't need to become a master; we need to be good enough to get a specific result in a limited time frame. I don't want to be the best. I want to be free.

Let me give an example of modeling. When I decided to create my first digital course, I researched online to determine who was the foremost authority on selling via webinars. There were a lot of courses and self-proclaimed gurus, but one name stood out among all of them. So I chose a training course by Mike Dillard, a well-respected online trainer who had made millions and whose students had become successful. I bought his course for $2,000, studied it religiously, and applied what I learned. I didn't go out and buy five courses; I only bought one from a master. I applied every single thing in that course to the tee. What I learned from him and modeled has now made me millions.

If you choose to leverage expert advice, you are taking the express highway to success. I once spent $17,000 to hang out with a guy who's a big OG in the marketing world named Frank Kern. He gave me one idea that changed my business overnight. It wasn't any kind of earth-shattering piece of advice, it was just an idea I wasn't executing on. Talking to him allowed me to forget about everything else and do the one thing that would take my business to the next level.

Here's how you can quickly determine your ROI using the modeling method. Use it to see if your investment in the expertise will be worth it. Is the money I'm going to spend with this master likely to pay me back at least what I invested in the next twelve months? If so, I break even on my investment, and get the knowledge for free. Yeah, that's the absolute worst case.

By the way, it almost never returns 1:1. It's often more like 1:5, 1:10, or 1:1,000,000. I'll say it here again: there are only two ways you lose by investing in others for their expertise. The first is if you do not do what they say. The second is if you do what they say, and it does not work. The first is on you, and the second is on you as well. Choose wisely.

How can we leverage the masters? It can be via books, courses, masterminds, events, coaching, in person, virtual, and more. Yes, there is a shortcut to success, despite what you've been told. That shortcut is modeling.

CONSUMERS GET POOR

PRODUCERS GET PAID

[18]

ARE YOU A PRODUCER OR A CONSUMER?

THERE ARE TWO SIDES TO every transaction. When money moves from one hand to another, value is exchanged. The person giving the money exchanges it for something that they believe is of equal or greater value than the cash they are giving up.

Most people only live on one side of this equation, as consumers. They are always giving money to get something, rather than being on the receiving end of money. These individuals aren't looking for opportunities to give value; they simply are looking to consume.

Here is why I want you to become a producer: producers get paid. When you go see a movie, you hand over $14 and get a couple of hours of entertainment (consumer). But the production company makes millions on the film (producer). When you call an Uber you get from point A to point B (consumer), but the dudes on the other end who created the app end up billionaires (producers).

Uber is number one in ridesharing and Lyft is number two, but who owns the sixth best ride hailing app in the world? Does it matter? That dude, even though he's a small producer compared to the big boys, likely earns more than 99 percent of the users on his app. See where I'm going here? Being a small-time producer still beats the pants off being a consumer.

Every wealthy person is a producer first and a consumer second. And when they do consume, they aren't doing it like you and me. They can afford to consume luxury homes, mega yachts, and jets. They get to consume at those levels because they've produced at even higher levels. They thrive and become super wealthy because they serve such a vast population of consumers.

So what does that look like in practical terms? How can you become a producer? Stop paying rent; collect it. Don't buy products, sell them. Read books and then write one. Don't become a freelancer, own a freelance website (the average freelancer makes $39,000, whereas Upwork is worth $1.5 billion). Don't become an employee, employ others (the average full-time worker makes $46,000 a year, versus the millions or billions that those who employ others make). Don't become a house cleaner, own a house cleaning company. By cleaning thirty-one homes a day with a team, you can make millions a year. In the coming chapters I'll show you multiple paths from which to choose so you can become a producer yourself.

[19]

YOUR ASS OR YOUR ASSETS

I SPENT MANY YEARS TRYING TO understand how people became wealthy. One of the reasons why some people thrive financially is because they rely on their assets to do most of the work. Your potential to earn income will always be limited, but assets have no limits on how much they can earn. If you want to play with unlimited income, you need to play with assets, and give your ass a break.

What is an asset? Well, there are various definitions depending on whom you ask. I'm going to avoid any definitions that have to do with accounting or the dry, boring world of finance. For the purpose of this book we are going to call an asset anything that passively puts money in our pocket. It's that simple.

 Rich people acquire assets. The poor and middle
class acquire liabilities that they think are assets."
—ROBERT KIYOSAKI

Some items could be considered assets, like a diamond ring, a vehicle, or even your house. But none of those "assets" put real, hard, spendable currency in your bank account. On the other hand, owning a business, dividend stocks, or investment properties are all examples of assets. They generate cash flow that goes into your pocket.

Why am I using this narrow definition of assets? Because the philosophy I'm sharing with you is based on creating the kind of income that requires little if any of your personal time. By focusing on acquiring only those kinds of assets, you can become immensely wealthy on both sides of the time-money matrix.

As we aim to find assets that can generate passive income for us, we should look at those who are doing it today and creating quick fortunes. Passivepreneurs are made up of creators, controllers, and owners. Let's dive in to learn about each one of these passivepreneur archetypes so we can decide which one we want to become.

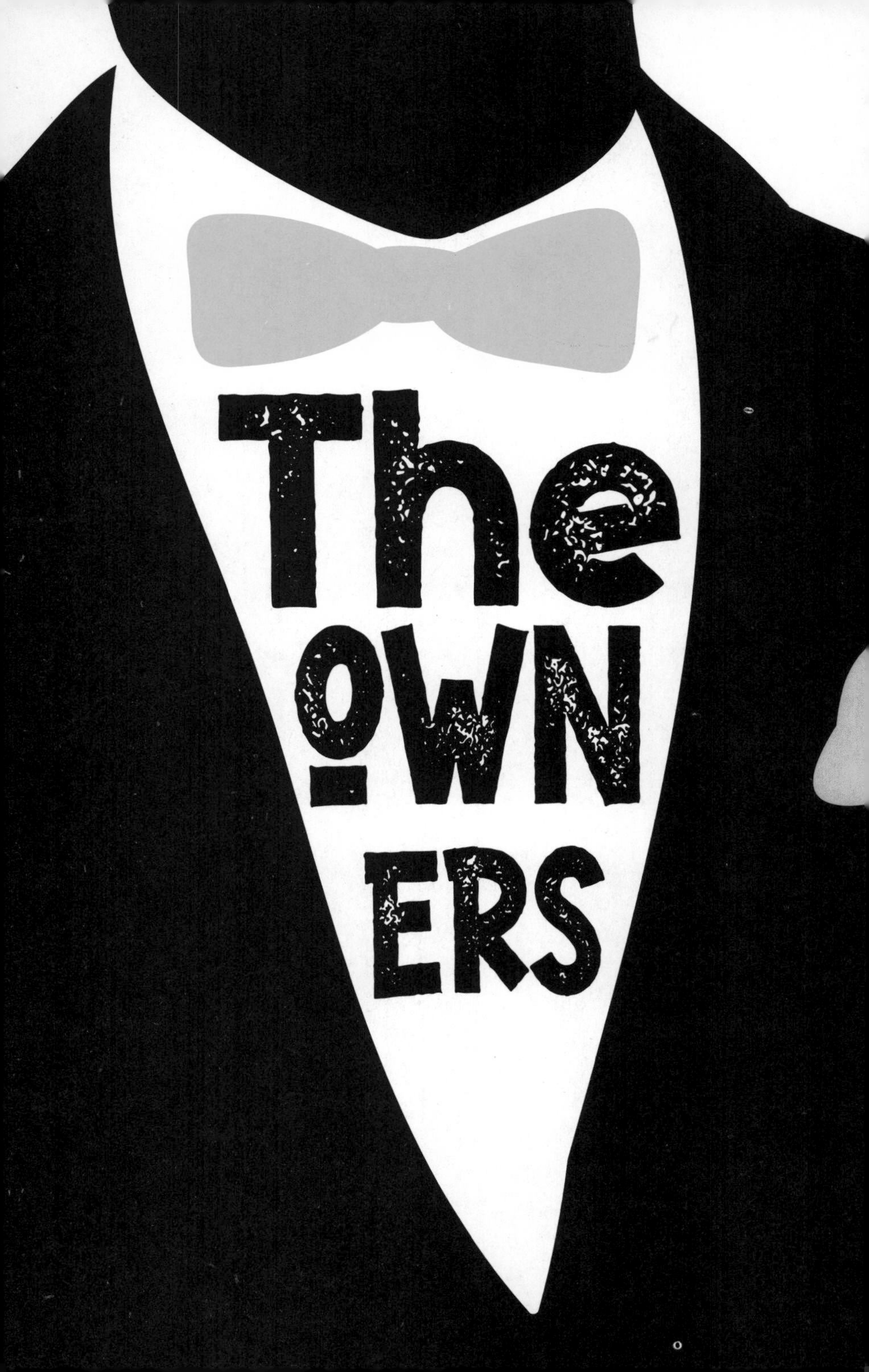
The
OWN
ERS

[20]

THE OWNER PASSIVEPRENEUR

OWNERS EXCHANGE THEIR OWN HARD-EARNED money or borrow money to purchase an asset in their name. If you are buying any asset that generates cash flow from day one, you are by definition an owner. This is a great way to get started quickly, and surprisingly doesn't always require use of your own funds.

For example, for my first real estate purchase after graduating from college, I decided to buy a duplex and live in one of the units. Because it was owner-occupied, I was able to get it for no money down. The other unit in the duplex had three bedrooms that I rented out individually to local college students. The income from those three rooms was enough to cover the mortgage and all the utilities, and still have a little bit left over for me in positive cash flow.

That duplex was an asset because it put money in my pocket. As a side benefit, it gave me a free place to live—indefinitely. I was the owner of this property, and my name was on the deed. Although I had a mortgage, I wasn't paying for it out of my own pocket. I went on to buy a lot more properties after that first duplex, but this was the first time that I stepped into the role of being an owner. Once I acquired enough rental properties, I was able to live off the cash flow and pivot away from needing a job.

Other examples of assets that owners buy include apartment buildings, mortgage notes, or even websites and other "digital real estate," which you can find on sites like Flippa.com. Owners may buy automated businesses like laundromats, car washes, Redboxes, billboards, or storage rentals—anything unmanned and brick-and-mortar. There are countless assets that qualify. Some famous owners include Warren Buffett, Magic Johnson, and the Walton family of Walmart fame.

There are also silent partnerships, which is my favorite form of ownership. It allows you to be an owner without being an operator. For example, you can invest as a limited partner in a real estate project and own a piece of the upside 100 percent passively.

I did this myself with a partner in the commercial real estate space and now I bring others on as silent partners to purchase multifamily properties across the country. We allow accredited investors to get a piece of our commercial real estate deals. They enjoy tax-free returns when we do cash-out refinancing on the properties and they get passive cash flow while they wait. Investing in this way is one of the most hands-off vehicles to generate upsize returns that I know of, and it's fully secured by real assets. If you're an accredited investor with at least $250,000 in available capital and want to learn more, visit www.thepagefund.com.

Owning a company would qualify someone as an owner, but only if they do not have a hand in the day-to-day operations. Remember, we're looking to get more time, not a job. Do not, under any circumstances, buy a business if you are going to be the one who runs it. It does not qualify as a true PIV. If you can invest a very limited amount of time in the business and it continues to grow without you, congrats! You're an owner.

There are also ways to make money as an owner using the sharing economy. You could "share" your money via peer-to-peer lending with companies like LendingClub.com. Have a backyard or undeveloped land not doing anything? Put it on HipCamp.com and people will pay you to use it for events. You can rent out all kinds of things you own, like your pool, garage, or extra storage on Spacer.com.

Own a car? List it as a rental on Turo, or wrap it on Wrapify and turn it into a moving billboard. You could make enough to cover the car payment, meaning a free car to drive. You can also share your home on VRBO or Airbnb, or your boat on boatsetter.com. Share what you own and rent it out to make money. We'll talk in way more depth about the sharing economy when we get to the chapter on controllers.

Wealthy people have always known that owning a jet or yacht doesn't have to be as expensive as you'd think. In fact, a friend of mine found a way to buy a jet and it costs him nothing to own. It's a moneymaking venture due to the income the jet produces as a charter.

There are some advantages and disadvantages of being an owner. The number-one advantage of becoming an owner is that you're able to shrink the time frame required to get your hands on income-producing assets. If you set out to buy an income-producing rental property, it may take a couple months of searching to identify the property and close on it. But the minute you own that property and have a tenant in place, you reap the benefits of the income from the asset. Owning assets—if done right—is owning near-instant cash flow.

The disadvantage of being an owner is that by definition you must purchase, and in order to purchase you need money. This cash may come from you if you have the ability to write a check. It may also come from someone else if you are able to find a partner or, more often, a lender. If you have little in the way of investable money or you don't possess the credit to borrow, then you may be at a distinct disadvantage. Also, with debt, there is always risk. I learned that the hard way in the real estate crash of 2008, going from millions in net worth to $1.3 million in the hole and losing everything. Today, I live completely debt-free—not a dime owed to anyone. The only exception I make is for debt I don't sign a personal guarantee for. That kind of debt can make you very, very rich!

Being an owner may not be where you begin, but I believe that eventually everyone should aim to own assets directly at some point in their financial journey.

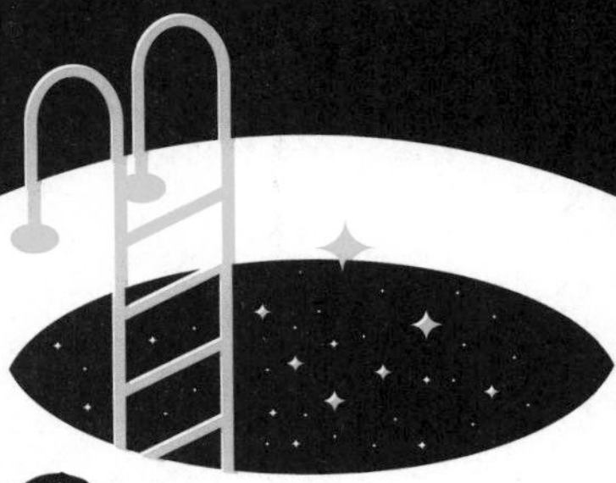

The CREATORS

[21]

THE CREATOR PASSIVEPRENEUR

FOR MANY, BECOMING A CREATOR is the easiest first step. This type of passivepreneur walks the path of "sweat equity" in order to bootstrap a business that has the potential to generate cash flow. It is possible to bypass the need to come up with much cash or ever use debt. Creators lean more on their own efforts and the powerful effect of exponential growth to help them become wealthy. Let's look more closely at this fast-growing group of passivepreneurs.

Creators are a different breed than owners. They often begin with no income, product, or service, and build something from the ground up using creativity and grit. This path may require long nights up front and a lot of working for free until you turn a profit. In fact, the vast majority of creators don't even turn a profit for many months or even years, depending on the industry. But the huge benefit of being a creator is that if they find a hit on their hands, they can become extremely wealthy. At the time of this writing, the wealthiest person in the world, Elon Musk, is one. Other famous creators include Jeff Bezos, Mark Zuckerberg, and Oprah Winfrey.

You don't need to make billions to become a creator. You simply need to generate passive income from what you create. You can do this creating paid content, online courses, digital products, platforms, software, apps, tech companies, and more. If you enjoy writing, you may choose to become an author and create a physical book, audiobook, or e-book. You can create digital products and courses or memberships where people pay you a monthly fee to be a part of your community. Podcasting can provide big sponsorship dollars if you build a big enough audience. The options are endless as a creator.

You can create software as a service (SaaS) or a mobile app where you collect a percentage every time someone makes a purchase. You may choose to become a content creator and host a show on YouTube. Want to become an influencer? You can endorse products on Instagram, making money via eyeballs you control through your digital persona. There is also consulting or coaching through group coaching or webinars.

You could create patents, rights, or licenses, or you may choose to get into private labeling: find great products and bring them to the market as your own brand. Creators have more opportunities today than ever before. It's no wonder many people choose to start as one.

Not only is it possible to make millions in a short amount of time as a creator, but it fits our definition of wealth perfectly. That's because once the asset is created, it has the potential to pay you over and again for many years.

The single biggest advantage of becoming a creator is that getting started takes little in the way of financial resources. A friend once asked me how much it would take them to launch a business online. They had witnessed me doing well with my online products and assumed that it must have cost a lot of money to do so. They were shocked to hear that at the time I launched my first product, I had only spent a few hundred dollars. I set up some online tools and spent about $800 to hire someone on Upwork to make them all work.

To become a successful creator myself took a limited amount of money but it required a lot of my own effort and time in the beginning. Sorry, there is no free lunch. Whether it's with money or time, you have to pay up.

That brings us to the biggest disadvantage of being a creator. You must have a significant amount of energy, focus, and personal time to become successful. In other words, if you're not afraid of some good old-fashioned hard work for a few years, you can generate significant cash flows as a creator.

However, you must be willing to invest continually over time, perhaps without seeing a direct result. It is not at all like being an owner where you buy it today and reap the rewards tomorrow. More like work today, tomorrow, and every day for the next few months or for years to be set for life.

To be honest, there's a high failure rate for most creators. It's estimated that 90 percent of all small businesses fail within the first five years. I would guess that number is even higher if you were to account for all the millions of people who set out to create a business but don't report their failures. So, if you're going to become a creator, you're going to have to give an enormous amount of yourself now to get much more time and money later. Yet I would tell you, it's very much worth the price.

I would encourage you to go this road as long as you're aware of what's required. A good part of this book addresses the qualities we need to develop to become a successful creator. Most importantly, we will look at the pitfalls that can prevent us from getting there. More on that in the last section of this book. Until then, let's move on to the final class of the passivepreneur—one that you might not be aware of.

THE CONTROLLERS

[22]

THE CONTROLLER PASSIVEPRENEUR

THE FINAL CLASS OF PASSIVEPRENEUR are the controllers. This little-known subset of business mavericks have learned how to generate passive income where it wouldn't seem any would exist. They are able to create cash flow from assets they don't own directly. They are able to leverage other people's assets for their own benefit.

Examples of controllers include affiliate marketers (who control and sell other people's products,) resellers who sell products they don't yet own, and even hedge fund managers, who control other people's money.

The whole concept of controlling assets was introduced to me in an unexpected way. Years ago when I was working for a marketing company, I was required to go to conferences around the country from time to time. During one of my regular trips, I was on a flight to Phoenix, sitting in business class. A gentleman sat next to me and introduced himself. I noticed the $30,000 Rolex on his wrist and his expensive-looking Italian shoes. The guy oozed success. He told me that he bought and sold companies and was an angel investor in several different industries. I told him that I was an aspiring entrepreneur who was struggling a bit to figure out what to do next after going through the big real estate crash.

I explained that years earlier in my twenties I had become a millionaire and enjoyed living off the cash flow that my rental properties generated. The only reason I had this job now was because I had to make ends meet, since I no longer owned any of those properties. I also told him how I had created a nice little income on Airbnb by putting the second bedroom in the apartment I rented on the site.

He proceeded to ask me more questions about my side business and how it worked. I couldn't figure out why this guy was asking so much about what I was doing. He couldn't be interested in doing Airbnb himself, I thought, being that he was making millions buying and selling companies. But he seemed genuinely interested.

After continuing our conversation for some time I finally asked him, "Why are you so interested in what I'm doing with Airbnb?"

He replied, "Because I think you might be on to something big here."

I asked with doubt in my voice, "Which part exactly?"

He took a sip of his coffee and looked at me intently. "Well, I think if you were to scale this thing and get a bunch of properties that it could be very lucrative."

I agreed with that logic. It would only take a few of these to replace my income from my job. But I already knew that was impossible.

"I can't scale this thing because I don't have the ability to buy properties anymore. In fact, even if I could, I don't think I would want to take that risk. I've been burned in the past by taking out a bunch of loans."

He looked at me and smiled. "Brian, it's not about owning, it's about controlling."

"What do you mean?"

He continued, "If you can legally control properties and use them to generate income, you don't need to own them. You simply lease the properties from the owners in a way that gives you legal control. You get their permission to put them online as short-term rentals. Granted, you wouldn't get the advantage of building equity, but that's not what you need right now. What you need is enough cash flow to be able to quit this job and go enjoy the lifestyle that you want."

When he spoke those words, it was like a light bulb went off in my head. I couldn't believe how such a simple idea had eluded me.

"So you're saying all I need to do is become a controller?" I offered.

"Yep, that's what I'm saying. Based on what you're telling me you're making from your spare room, it wouldn't take many properties to generate a significant income."

A few days later I was on the plane home and filled with a new-found sense of hope. I did exactly what he suggested. The funny thing was, I was able to become financially free faster as a controller than I did when I was an owner. In my twenties it took three years, a bunch of mortgages, and millions of dollars of real estate. As a controller it took none of the above.

Within six months I was in a position to walk away from my six-figure job—all from five properties. I quit my job and went on to get many more properties and scale my business. This one vehicle allowed me to become free of a job for life. It gave me the time I needed to live the lifestyle I'd always dreamed of. It also put me on track to building real wealth from many other PIVs. Becoming an Airbnb controller gave me a second chance to get back all I had lost and so much more. I now have a group coaching program where my six-figure BNB coaches show people exactly how to do this. To this day I don't know of an easier, quicker PIV to create cash flow than through Airbnb. You can find out more at www.freebnbcall.com.

Being a controller allowed me to enjoy the fruit of being an owner without having any of the resources of one. It's a very powerful model because all it takes is relationship capital. Simply enroll someone on the idea that by you controlling their assets, it's a win-win for both of you. It is possible to help property owners make more money with less work while at the same time creating an ethical and very lucrative source of revenue for yourself.

Here's another example of a controller. My friend Randy lists his friends' cars on Turo, a car sharing app. He gives them a part of the revenue those cars generate. He's created a nice income for himself, and now has it all on autopilot—with cars he controls via his profit-sharing agreement. He owns nothing and he created nothing, but he has cash flow.

Affiliate marketers also fall into this category. Affiliate marketers have the right to sell someone else's products and services. As an example, I allow affiliates to sell my products (if they meet certain requirements). Any sales they generate are split 50/50 with them. Think about that for a second. They created nothing, they don't own the product, they spent nothing up front, and yet they can make a bundle from controlling the right to sell my products. I have affiliates with a big email list who have made over $100,000 in a weekend doing this. Grant Cardone inadvertently sold over six figures for me by posting an interview of us on YouTube. I promptly cut him a check for half of those sales the next time I sat down with him in Miami.

You can control attention. For example, as an affiliate, if you redirect people from your website via links to products you recommend on Amazon, you can make a commission each time they click and buy. Controlling attention is an incredibly lucrative way to generate wealth. Influencers do this all the time. They control where their followers focus and they can direct that traffic to products and offers from which they themselves benefit.

I do this all the time with amazing companies I support. In fact, I have links to some of them right here in this book. You better believe I practice what I preach! Each of those services is another PIV spewing money my way. Here's how it works: I control attention through this book and use that attention to create cash flow. I did not create, nor do I own, the services or products I'm sharing; I simply control eyeballs. There's no reason you can't do the same.

Multilevel marketing or network marketing is another great way to become a controller. You might not own the company you represent, but you leverage their platform to generate passive income. You control the network and how many people are in your downline. Ultimately, whoever controls the biggest team earns the most.

Drop shippers are one of my favorite and most overlooked types of controllers. They use a business model that allows them to build a virtual storefront. They then sell to the public without the need to buy, manufacture, create, own, or even deliver products. A lot of people do this on Shopify or Amazon. You can control the flow of buyers to your storefront without creating or owning anything! Cool.

In fact, the next time you buy something online, even from a big company brand you recognize, look closer. The brand you love might simply be forwarding your order to a factory or wholesaler and taking a cut. You think Amazon has a factory somewhere that churns out all their branded products? Nope. They're just one very, very big controller. Do they own or create the products on their site? Nope again. They control the traffic of the hundreds of millions who visit the site.

Being a controller wasn't possible in many industries until recently. For example, with Airbnb, the ability to do rental arbitrage didn't even exist until the company was launched, which was not many years ago. There was no easy way to earn short-term income on a long-term property. As soon as a platform was set up that managed the bookings, payments, and all the logistics for hosts, an opportunity emerged. Anyone with the desire to launch a listing on the site could now generate income for themselves. Technology is opening up more opportunities every day to control assets.

The beauty of becoming a controller is this: assets don't care. A property doesn't care if the person who's collecting money on Airbnb is me or the owner. It doesn't care if I make more than the owner does, and it doesn't spit off less income because I am now in control.

The simple takeaway here is you don't need to be the owner of an asset to profit from it. You simply need to control the asset. So, if you like the idea of ethically hacking income streams owned by someone else, becoming a controller may be for you. It can be your shortcut to creating passive income for yourself in the shortest amount of time possible.

Which type of passivepreneur should you become? Let's see. Do you like building and bringing something to life over time? Maybe you should be a creator. Are you good at negotiating with people and building trust? You should be a controller. Do you like to collect things or have the ability to write big checks? Then you're an owner. You may start off as any one of these types of passivepreneurs, but you are not limited to one.

Here's what my own journey as a passivepreneur looks like. I became an owner first in my twenties (real estate), a controller next (short-term rentals), and a creator third (digital marketer). I kept repeating the process. I launched a real estate fund (controller), wrote books (creator), partnered on commercial properties (owner), launched a consulting company (owner), and more. I now have dozens of PIVs and am always on the lookout for more. By the way, do you know of one I haven't mentioned in this book? Direct message me on any of the social channels (my handle is @bpagester). I'm always looking to learn more PIVs and share them with readers.

To recap: owners buy assets, creators build assets, and controllers leverage assets they don't own. Once you buy, build, or leverage assets, you, too, will be a passivepreneur. Want a list of the best passive income ideas available today? I got them for you at www.dontstartasidehustle.com/resources.

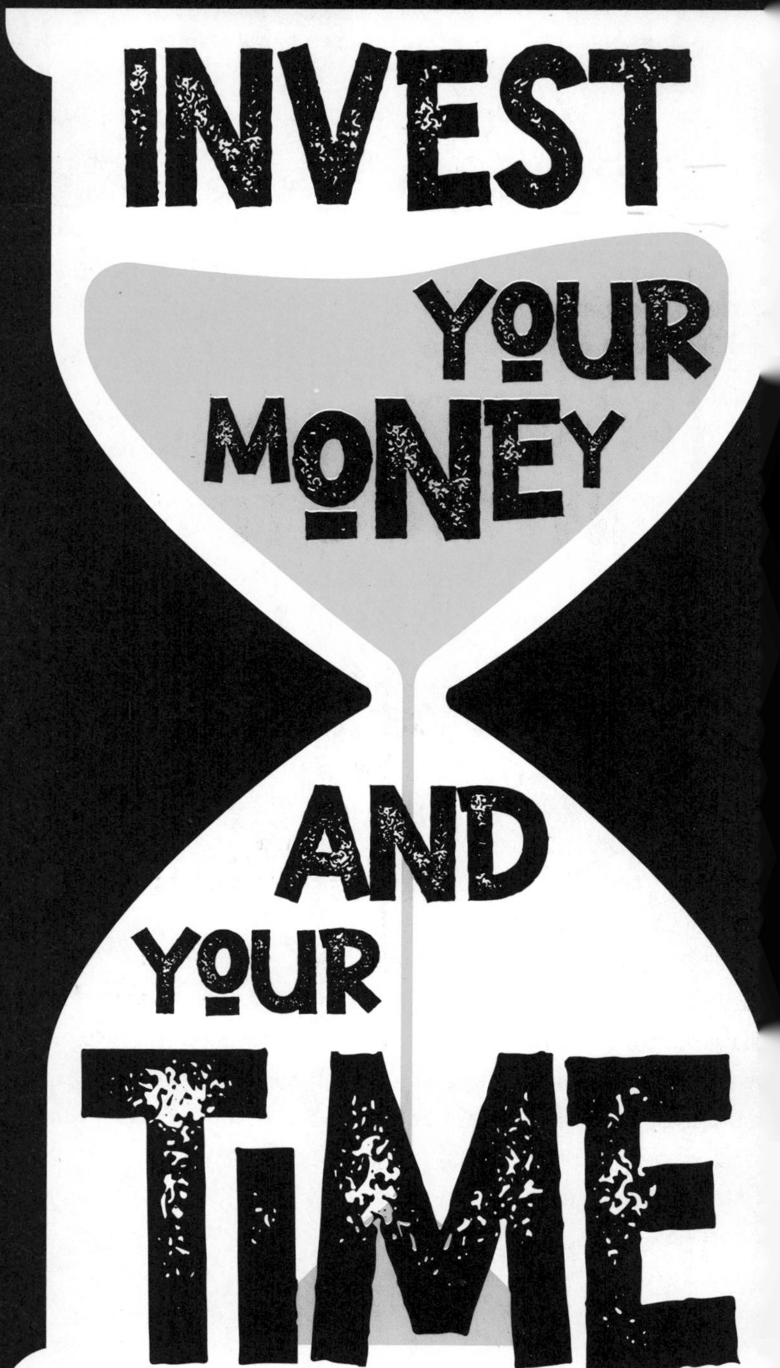
INVEST
YOUR
MONEY
AND
YOUR
TIME

[23]

THE DIFFERENCE BETWEEN TRADING AND INVESTING TIME

MOST OF US GROW UP with the expectation that we will get a formal education at a college or university that will lead to a well-paying, safe, secure job. We don't go to a job or build a career for free, we do it because we are compensated. Sadly, the most logical way to be compensated (as we are taught) is to trade our time for it.

One thing that we are generally not told about this trade is that our income will always be limited because the time that we have available to earn it is limited. For example, if tomorrow we set out to make ten times or a hundred times more money next month at our job than we made this month, we can't raise our working hours a hundred- or thousandfold.

Not only is our time-tied income not scalable, but we also need to consider the fact that the moment we stop working is the moment our income stops. The trade is directly proportional. The saying that best encapsulates this agreement is, "You don't work, you don't eat." It's something I heard regularly growing up.

Pay that is tied to time is a dead end if you plan to become a passivepreneur. Time-based income is linear and doesn't have the power to produce wealth rapidly. There are some exceptions, of course. For example, a top draft pick for the NBA gets a $12 million signing bonus or a billion-dollar company hires a high-priced CEO. But if you're in that envious situation, I doubt you're reading this book.

If we opt out of trading our time for money and doing work that is unscalable, what is the solution? The solution is to invest our time. We must invest as much of our limited time as we can into activities that either generate passive income or have the potential to.

 Your salary is the bribe they give you to forget your dreams."

— CHRISJAN (CJ) PETERS

"But, Brian, how am I going to do that?" you might ask. "I have a job! It's not like I'm broke, but I have no time. How do I invest my time if I have so little of it?" The reality is that until you've invested enough time into passive income–producing activities, you may still need to work that job. If you spend eight hours a day there and eight hours a night sleeping, you must carve out as many of the other eight hours in the day as possible to devote to building your wealth creation vehicle.

I was in this scenario a few years ago as I juggled my full-time job and my Airbnb business. I would spend my days at work (often for up to twelve hours) and my nights and weekends putting any leftover moments into my PIV. It wasn't easy. I had little time for socializing or dating or relaxing in front of the TV. But I knew that by sacrificing my time and investing it (not trading it), eventually I would be able to kick the job to the curb. When I did, I went from working fifty-plus hours to five hours a week. The time I invested has come back to pay me *huge* dividends, and the time I invested in the past is now returned to me—with interest!

[24]

HOW TO WORK ONCE AND GET PAID FOREVER

BESIDES FALLING INTO THE TRAP of trading our time for money, we also may fall for the idea of getting paid once. For example, if I put in a week's worth of work, I get paid for a week. If I work a year, I get paid a salary for that year. If I complete a big project or a gig for which I am paid a certain fee, no matter how much I may take home, I am only going to be paid once.

The simplest test to know if you're paid once is this: if you stop doing the income-producing activity and your pay stops, you are being paid once. A surgeon may make $400,000 a year, but I don't know of many who still get paid if they stop showing up to work.

Here's the cruel reality of getting paid once. The only way you can get ahead and make quantum leaps in your level of wealth is to work longer! Rarely do we stop to consider what our return on time (ROT) is. However, if we spend our time and then are paid over and over, that ROT is infinite! Every additional sale of my online course means the amount I make for each hour invested keeps going up. So long as that asset I created generates income, my dollars per hour keep climbing. Imagine making tens of thousands of dollars per hour. That can't happen when you're paid once.

What's the alternative to being paid once? Being paid many times! Here's the test: if you stop the income-producing activity but your income does not, you are getting paid many times. For example, I put in a lot of time and energy creating my first software tool three years ago. But when I put it up for sale and automated the process I got paid many times, and still get paid every day for that work even now, years later.

The reason you must get clear on whether you are getting paid once or many times is because there is always a temptation to try and make more money. Perhaps you said it yourself or to your friends:

"I need to get some overtime."

"I need a raise."

"I need a second job."

"I need a job that pays better!"

These are all logical answers if your question is, "How do I make more money?" But there's a problem with this approach: although the answers above are all valid, the question itself is wrong.

Instead of asking, "How can I make more money?" a much more powerful question is, "How can I make more *recurring* money?" Ask, "How can I earn many times over from that one time I've worked?" Ask, "How can my hour be worth $100, $1,000, or $10,000 and keep growing?" Those are the questions we should ask.

ARE YOU TOO BUSY

TO BE PRODUCTIVE?

[25]

HOW TO FOREVER AVOID UNPRODUCTIVE BUSYNESS

OKAY, SO YOU'RE NOW FULLY on board with investing your time rather than trading it. You're committed to looking for ways to get paid many times for your hours rather than getting paid only once. But there's one more question you must ask yourself every day so that you don't fall into the biggest time waster (and wealth stealer) of all.

Have you ever gotten to the end of your workday and felt like you're not sure what, if anything, you accomplished? Maybe your day was filled with a flurry of to-do's and multitasking. Maybe you've had a string of these kinds of days for weeks or months, but don't have that sense that you're getting any closer to achieving your goals. You're doing a ton, but not getting much back. The reason for this is because you're busy.

"Well, duh, Brian, of course I'm busy. Who isn't?"

Here's the distinction: being busy is what prevents us from being productive. What is the difference between the two? Productive actions are those that get us closer to our goal. Being busy is spending your time getting *more* done; productivity is getting the *right* things done. I would argue that it is only the right things that ultimately matter. In fact, you could be highly productive but not all that busy! Let me show you how.

A shortcut to being incredibly productive is to identify whether you are conscious or unconscious about your to-do's. Consciousness, in this context, means not only being aware of what we need to do, but being aware of whether or not we are effectively executing on what we need to do in any given moment.

Most of us go through our day simply choosing whatever is next the moment we start doing that activity. It may involve putting out fires, or something lands in our laps, or our inbox lures us back to check it again. We move from one task to the next with no structure or plan. We may even get a high from this kind of activity; we feel super important and accomplished when we can make a list and check it off.

Here's the thing. Rarely do you completely finish your to-do list. It just continually gets filled up again with new things that we need to address. Just as you can remain in poverty by spending your money and never investing it, you can also experience time poverty by getting trapped in staying busy. So what's the solution? To be conscious of what is most important to do right now in this moment and to be aware of whether we are doing it.

So how do we define what's important? The easiest way to identify important tasks is to ask yourself if completing those tasks gets you closer to your ultimate goal. Often, the items that we least want to do are the ones that we most need to. In the same way many of the things we most like to do are the ones we need to avoid or delay doing.

The best way I've found to get over the reluctance to knock things out is developing the habit of doing the hard things first.

Putting off actions that are complex and require a lot of thinking or energy does not make those tasks easier to complete later. I wrote about this idea of time blocking already if you remember.

Again, let me talk about my experience writing this book. When I come into my office at the beginning of the day, I don't look at my to-do list. I don't check emails or voicemails or messages. I put my phone on airplane mode. I put a Do Not Disturb sign outside my office and I don't answer the door if someone shows up. From that block of time from 9:00 a.m. to noon, I'm relentlessly focused. That's it: three hours. And because of that ability to focus, it's amazing what can be accomplished.

When that time is over, I come up for air knowing that, for the rest of the day, it doesn't matter what things I want to do next. I've become so disciplined about giving my best hours to what's important and doing so every single day that I can be less structured in the second half of the day. Heck, I can even be busy if I feel like it! As one of my mentors once taught me, "Brian, once you do what is most important for the day, you can go home, no matter what time it is."

What if that were a regular occurrence for you? Imagine leaving work early because you know that you are on track to achieve your highest objectives. Instead of going home feeling like you had a busy day, you go home feeling like a rock star. You entered a state of flow where you were consciously enjoying the journey of success.

[26]

PASSIVE INCOME VEHICLES (PIVs)

LOVE OR HATE HER, KYLIE Jenner is a sign of the times when it comes to wealth creation. As one of the youngest billionaires (or near billionaire depending on whom you ask), she is the perfect example of how wealth is being created at astronomical levels in very short amounts of time.

A century ago it took sixty years for Andrew Carnegie to become a billionaire. It took two decades for Ross Perot to do it in the 1970s. In the "greed is good" era of the '80s, Bill Gates did it in a decade. Snapchat CEO Evan Spiegel reached that level in less than four years. As of the time of this writing, twenty billionaires have done so in less than three years. Three years to a freaking billion. And a billionaire is minted every twenty-three hours. That's mind bending.

Immense wealth is being created quicker than ever and the trend is also accelerating at the "merely" millionaire level. So when I say it's possible to walk away from your job in a few months or become a millionaire in less than a year, I want you to know that it is actually possible.

I want to share an analogy to help you better understand the importance of choosing the right vehicle. As I go through this analogy, I want you to think of hours as years. Imagine you need to get from New York to Los Angeles. Starting in the first city is analogous to the day that you choose to become a passivepreneur. When you arrive on the West Coast is when you've achieved your passive income goal.

Let's say you have the insane idea to run from one coast to the other, Forrest Gump style. The world record for doing this incredible feat is forty-two days and six hours, set by Pete Kostelnick in 2016. This feat is only possible by individuals with herculean levels of endurance and perseverance. Even if it took you ten times longer to walk across the country, most anyone could do it if they had the desire. An overweight nonrunner named Steve Vaught did just that and wrote a book about it called *Fat Man Walking.*

So with enough desire we might be able to do it, but most of us would run out of life before we arrived at our destination. The biggest challenge in this walking/running scenario is that there is no leverage. Every aspect of moving under your own power across this continent is 100 percent reliant on your own body, willpower, and effort. I want you to think about this mode of transportation as equal to working a minimum-wage job. This individual may be hardworking and earnest and have huge dreams, but they will likely never achieve them, simply due to their vehicle.

A better vehicle would be one that allows you to use some leverage. The world record for cycling across the country was set in 2014 by Christoph Strasser who crossed the continent in an astonishing seven days and twenty-two hours. This is a fivefold improvement over running. It's only possible because of the gears of the bicycle compounding the efforts of one's muscle movement.

Many people believe that, if they have some form of leverage and they are getting to their destination faster, they are on the right track. They look at the runner they blew past and think, *Dang, I'm glad I'm not that guy!* They may look good; they have their head-to-toe spandex on; they may be channeling their inner Lance Armstrong. Their bike is made out of carbon fiber, and they have all the latest gear. They feel like they have a real good shot at arriving at the other side. Sadly, few will ever complete the trip. Three out of every four Americans die with no savings and with an average of $62,000 in debt. Think of this individual as a working-class person who has a decent job.

Okay, you're smarter than the cyclist. You decide to grab a comfy luxury car, jump in, and set out on the forty-hour cross-country drive. This is what I call a forty-year plan. It's the one that almost everyone buys into, and it goes like this: *If I commit the next thirty to forty years of my life to a career and set aside a little bit of money each paycheck, one day I'll be able to retire.* It's the saver's vehicle.

These well-employed people with decent jobs were sure they had the right vehicle. In fact, most people admired the car that they were driving and gave them the thumbs-up as they drove by. They went to school for many years and got the cool degree to be able to get into such a car. They obsess about cars and talk about them and compare their cars to other people's cars. What they don't know is their vehicle of choice is still 100 percent reliant on them. If they stop driving, then that car will go nowhere. If they get into an accident along the way, or fall asleep at the wheel, the entire trip is off. This type of person is generally the educated middle class.

At this point in the analogy, you may be reading this and thinking, *The answer is obvious. Why not just get on a plane and fly to Los Angeles?* It is a great option. So why do millions of people still choose to drive this route every day? If you took away any desire to experience the open road or traveling for the purpose of sightseeing, why would anybody not choose to fly? Well, there are many reasons.

For some it could be the fear of flying, for others perhaps the cost, and for others it might simply be because nobody they know flies. In this analogy, we can compare flying to becoming a passive-preneur. The difference between flying and using any other vehicle to cross the country is that with flying you are not only leveraging tools and the vehicle you are in, but you are also leveraging the efforts of other people.

When you drive a car, there's only one person needed to operate that vehicle. When you jump on a plane, you are leveraging the massive resources of the airline to help you get to your destination much, much faster. There are flight attendants, baggage handlers, maintenance crews, air traffic controllers, pilots, and countless other individuals you will never see who make that trip possible.

And the best part of using this vehicle is that you can sit back and spend your time doing other productive activities while you fly. You are making constant progress toward your destination while using your time for whatever you choose. In fact, while en route you could be planning future trips. Getting on a plane is not unlike being a passivepreneur. This superior vehicle can get you to your destination in five hours or less, which is a tenfold improvement over any of the slower vehicles. Who wouldn't want to fly?

This is the point in the story where most people say, "That's me!" You're sitting up in coach or first class sipping coffee. You look 30,000 feet below to all the poor souls who are creeping along like ants on the highway. You're blitzing at 600 miles an hour and feeling pretty good about yourself. What could be better? You think, *Yeah, maybe I could be flying private, but this is pretty cool. I'm going as fast as possible.* But is that true?

The SR 71 Blackbird holds the record for the fastest manned aircraft. It flew from coast to coast in sixty-four minutes. In fact, the plane was so fast that the air it pushed in front of it didn't have time to get out of the way. It would build up such a high temperature, the engineers had to design gaps in the metal frame. When the plane got up to speed, those gaps expanded due to the intense heat, and the plane sealed itself. The Blackbird would leak fuel as it sat on the runway awaiting takeoff. Insane, right? But there are always faster vehicles.

Is supersonic flight the upper limit of how fast humans can travel? Well, the future would say no. We are on the cusp of entering commercial suborbital flight. What is suborbital? Imagine speeds that are so fast it would take just a few minutes to go from one side of the country to the other. You wouldn't even have time for your complimentary in-flight drink before the wheels touched down in LA.

Suborbital flight is so fast you could go from one side of the globe to the exact opposite side (12,000 miles) in less than the time it took that supersonic Blackbird to go across the United States. There would be no need for a lavatory on board, in-flight entertainment, or meals. It would take you longer to get from the entrance of the airport to your departing gate than it would to go across the continent. Sheesh.

How are such speeds even possible? A traditional aircraft is limited by physics, because as it flies, it needs to push the air in front of it out of the way as well as create lift to overcome the constant pull of gravity. Those two forces make it mathematically impossible to go faster than a certain speed. But once you enter space, the entire game changes. This vehicle is traveling through space rather than through air as it goes around the planet.

You may be thinking that this is the stuff of science fiction, but companies like Blue Origin by Jeff Bezos, SpaceX by Elon Musk, and even Virgin Galactic by Richard Branson are all working to make this mainstream. It's only a matter of time before this will become available to consumers. When that day arrives, it will be such a radical change in travel that it would be similar to the 1950s when commercial flights first became available to the masses. There will be a day when people who have the ability to write the check can travel at such speeds. Somebody take my money!

So what's the point of this analogy? Simply this: there is always a faster vehicle. Vehicles are changing and becoming obsolete. Immense wealth is being created in the cryptocurrency space, for example, and it isn't even a ten-year-old technology. When you get to a certain point on your passivepreneur journey, you will be able to identify faster and faster vehicles. If you keep your eyes open and have a belief that they exist, you will find more openings to take advantage of these vehicles. It's important to remember that you and your efforts don't matter nearly as much as the vehicle you choose to take the journey in.

I believe that in the future wealth will be created at increasing levels and shorter time frames. In the not-too-distant future, we will see the world's first trillionaire. The number of people who are creating wealth today is astounding—even if you consider the world's 46 million garden-variety millionaires. This is a telltale sign that there will be even more tomorrow. The velocity and speed at which wealth can be created is limited only by the vehicle one is in.

What I want you to take from this is that we must make sure that the speed our vehicle is capable of maintaining is factored into your timeline. If it isn't, be open to choosing a better one. Don't expect that if you're driving across the country that you can go ten times faster simply by hitting the accelerator. Don't think that if you walk up to the pilot and ask them to lay the hammer down that they can make that 747 arrive in half the time. Be aware that there's always another level and another possibility.

Your destination might be $10,000 a month. It might be six figures a day. Perhaps it's becoming the next billionaire. Whatever it is for you, the vehicle you choose is the first and most important consideration. Our goal is to get to the destination as quickly as possible with the most life left over to enjoy it.

≈≈≈ 100110
1001101110
DIGITAL
IS THE NEW
ANALOG

[27]

CHOOSING YOUR FIRST PIV

THERE ARE A TON OF both analog (brick-and-mortar) and digital (online) opportunities from which you can build wealth. In the analog sphere, you could invent a product, write a book, own something physical like a car wash, laundromat, or billboards, and even sell advertisements over urinals. ("Need a prostate exam? Call us!")

Analog opportunities are often the ones that our parents may have pursued or encouraged us to look into. They are easy to recognize and generally exist in the traditional business world. If you can touch it, smell it, see it, and hold it in your hands, it's analog. Think of brick-and-mortar stores, physical products, and even services you can experience in person, like going to the movies, getting a massage or a haircut, flying, or going to a restaurant.

Traditionally, people have built wealth via analog assets in the physical world. But the digital realm is where the biggest up-and-coming opportunities are. It's where wealth is being created disproportionately. In my mind, this is where some of the greatest opportunities exist today.

In the digital sphere, the options are endless. They include anything that is not physical in nature. If it can be done via a screen (laptop, phone, tablet), it's digital. Think about companies in Silicon Valley like Google, Amazon, or Facebook. If you break it down to its simplest terms, they make money from pushing ones and zeroes through screens on our devices. Yes, like Amazon, they may sell physical products. But if you were to take away the screen, they would have no business model. What is Facebook when you're on airplane mode? What is Google without the internet? When you go buy a burrito at Chipotle, you can do so without ever connecting on mobile or online; just drive over and fill your belly. (This is changing rapidly as we speak due to food delivery apps like Grubhub and Uber Eats, but you get my point.)

Every business model from the past that can be done digitally is either moving that way or already has. For example, the entire financial industry—which includes stocks and securities, but also sexier and more recent breakthroughs like cryptocurrency and digital assets—is now digital.

Doubt me? Look at every company worth over a trillion dollars. How many of them would you place in the analog category? Saudi Aramco, an oil and gas company, is the only one, and we all know where that industry is headed.

RANK	COMPANY	SECTOR	MARKET CAP (IN US DOLLARS)
1	Apple	Technology	2.8 trillion
2	Microsoft	Technology	2.3 trillion
3	Saudi Aramco	Energy	1.9 trillion
4	Alphabet	Technology	1.8 trillion
5	Amazon	E-commerce/Tech	1.6 trillion
6	Tesla	Consumer	1.0 trillion
7	Meta	Technology	1.0 trillion

Source: CompaniesMarketCap.com

Compare this modern list to the seven most valuable companies in 1972. The leaders were General Motors, Exxon, Ford, General Electric, IBM, Mobil, and Chrysler. The story is clear: a disproportionate share of wealth is being created in the digital space, and not only with the world's most valuable companies.

The single most sexy thing about opportunities in the digital space is that they are open to nearly anyone. If you're one of the 4.66 billion people who have internet access, you can take part. You don't need to move to a new town; heck, you may not even need to leave the couch. When you crack the code to making money online, you can go anywhere and live a true laptop lifestyle.

OWNERS.

CREATORS.

CONTROLLERS.

[28]

EXAMPLES
OF PIVs

TO LIST OUT EVERY TYPE of passive income vehicle would take more space than this book allows, and that's a good thing. You will never be at a loss for vehicles if you know where to look. Let's go over a few here so we can narrow the list to one that we can launch in the next thirty days.

SPONSORSHIPS AND ENDORSEMENTS

Sponsorships occur when you have an audience of a certain size, like an email list or follower count on social media. An advertiser may offer to pay you to promote their products. You give a recommendation for the product or service in exchange for a payment.

With more than a million followers on Instagram, almost weekly I'm offered money in exchange for mentioning a product or service. The only work involved for me is to create a video or an audio talking about that product. It's the perfect example of working once and getting paid many times.

The only caveat here is that you need to be careful to only sponsor companies that are related to what you're about. If you're known for helping people in the fitness arena and suddenly you're doing sponsorships for Hardees, that might not be aligned with your audience. In the same vein, if you're recommending a company that takes advantage of people and has a horrible reputation, that can harm your brand and reputation. However, if the offer is aligned with your values and your audience, it can be a very good PIV.

TEMPLATES, SPREADSHEETS, AND CHECKLISTS

You might be surprised to learn that you can create simple tools in Google Sheets for zero dollars and sell them online to consumers. The key to selling these kinds of tools is to provide a solution to the buyer that makes getting the result they're after quicker or easier.

As an example, I recently purchased a spreadsheet that helps me calculate the profitability in one of my companies. It takes every single product that we have and calculates what it costs us to deliver each of them, compared to what it costs us to acquire a customer. I heard good things about this tool and gladly paid $49 for it.

When I got access, I realized that it was nothing more than a Google Sheet, but I didn't care. For me it was worth what I paid because not only did this tool save me countless hours but it gave me insight into my finances that I've never had before. It was created by someone I respected who had much more knowledge of analyzing numbers than I did. That individual has done more than $472,000 in sales just for this one spreadsheet. Crazy, right?

DIGITAL INTERACTIVE TOOLS
AND CALCULATORS

One of the products that I sell is called the BNB Deal Analyzer. Essentially, it's a glorified calculator that allows people to figure out what they will make on an Airbnb listing after all expenses. That may seem like a simple thing to figure out, but it's complex. When I first launched my Airbnb business, I had a hard time figuring out how to forecast what I would make on a property. There were so many variables that went into the equation. For example, I was charging a different price for every night of the week. Then I had to pay the cleaners and the fees to Airbnb. I had to pay for the rent on the property and the utilities and the virtual assistant that managed my listings. There are a lot of moving pieces, and if you didn't calculate one correctly, you had to start all over again. On top of all that, you couldn't change one variable such as what you charge on a Tuesday and be able to see immediately how it would affect what you made at the end of the month.

So I hired a software engineer to come up with a simple-to-read dashboard with easy-to-use dials. I told him I wanted to know the daily, monthly, and annual profitability on any property and be able to add in any custom expenses that I chose. I built what I needed. It cost me about $1,200 and took several months to get it right. But when it was done, there was nothing else like it available anywhere. I immediately went out to sell this product to people in the Airbnb space. To this day, that product has passively generated multiple six figures in sales and is used by thousands of people. And the most important thing? Since the day I created it two years ago, I put zero time into managing that PIV. Not one minute.

I've seen calculators for stock trading, flipping houses, commercial real estate analysis, and managing diet regimens. The sky's the limit for creating one of these cash cows.

SCALABLE SERVICES

This category of income-producing assets is anything that can be delivered to the consumer that isn't a physical or digital product. The key distinction here is that it can't be a service that is one-to-one.

For example, when you hire an accountant, he or she is going to charge you for their time and sell you their service. It may be scalable to the degree that they have other accountants in their office, but they're going to hit a hard limit at some point because they're selling their service one-to-one.

The opposite of this would be selling a service that is scalable. For example, one of my friends has a virtual assistant (VA) company. Essentially what he does is help entrepreneurs who don't want to spend the money to hire someone full-time. They would rather pay for each hour of time for a virtual worker and have the person work based on what is needed that particular week.

My friend can get an unlimited number of VAs from overseas and mark up their labor to sell to the end user. Since he has somebody who manages all of these VAs, not only is he able to scale, but he can do it without any direct intervention. Find a service that is scalable and not dependent on you to manage and put that PIV in your corner.

DIGITAL COURSES

I have a special place in my heart for digital courses. To this day they remain one of my most consistent PIVs and can be structured to be completely hands-off, if done correctly.

Online courses are all about selling information. In my opinion that is the best product you can sell. It doesn't require inventory or packaging. You don't have to ship it anywhere. Your customer gets it instantly after they purchase, and it can be sold 100 percent on autopilot.

How do you decide what to create a course on? There are two ways. You can go the route of teaching what you know and sharing your expertise—like real estate, in my case. You can also set out to become an expert on a topic and teach what you've learned in the process. The most important thing to consider is that if you're not yet an expert, you need to apply what you're teaching to make sure it produces results. It's not enough to be an academic if you want to sell a product that helps people. You need to take your own medicine by attempting to put into practice all the things you've learned and report on your results.

Let me give you an example. Let's say you're creating a course on dog training. You are by no means an expert on that topic. So you read every book that you can on dog training, and you consult the experts. Maybe you even go through some courses yourself. In time you'll know a lot. It would be safe to say you may know more about dog training than 99 percent of the population. Great! Now take what you've learned and distill it down into your own way of saying things (create your own model) and attempt to use it to train dogs! You can show within that course the results you've gotten using the model you came up with.

DIVIDEND STOCKS

Some companies distribute a part of their profits to all the shareholders. This is one of the easiest passive income sources available. Once you buy the dividend-paying stock, there's nothing else to be done. These dividends continue to roll in and can be leveraged back into more stock purchases or withdrawn as income. You can pick stocks individually or even invest in dividend-paying funds, which is essentially a group of stocks.

WHITE LABEL PRODUCTS

White labeling is a great way to control assets. The perfect example of this is Amazon-branded products. Most people are surprised to see how many different products they can buy on the site that have that Amazon logo on them. But here's the secret that most people don't know: Amazon doesn't create any of those products; they simply have permission to brand them as their own.

Here's a story you may find shocking. There's a company out there called Luxottica that manufactures over 90 percent of all sunglasses on the planet. That means that when you buy sunglasses—whether it's Oakley or Ray-Ban or Prada or the junky ones at the local gas station—there's a good chance that they were created by Luxottica. They are then branded with the name that you're familiar with. Crazy, right?

Not only can you create your own brand reselling a manufacturer's product in your own packaging, but you can also use drop shipping. This method of controlling assets is where items purchased by the end user are shipped directly from the manufacturer. You have no need for warehouses, no shipping center, no employees. It's all done for you. You control the marketing and sale of the product and a thirdparty drop shipper takes care of the rest. You'd be surprised how many brands are white labeling products that they didn't create—and there's no reason you can't do the same.

EMBEDDED OFFERS

Embedded offers are when a product or service is within another product or service already purchased by the user. For example, when you buy an iPhone and go to the App Store, every time you click on an app and buy something, Apple gets half of that fee. The app is embedded in the iPhone, which is the product the user paid for.

I've used this in my online course. People who are going through my training need to set up their own LLC or company in the process. I used to send them to websites like LegalZoom where they could do it themselves, until one day I was approached by a gentleman who made me an incredible proposal. He owned a company called PCS that sets up entities for people and he offered to set them up for my students. He offered to jump on a free consulting call with any of my students to help them set up an LLC or corporation in order to pay the least amount possible in taxes. This would save each student hundreds of dollars right out of the gate, giving them something they needed anyway. He offered other services like tax consulting that people could choose to add on, which is how he was able to do this for free. He suggested making an offer within my course with a button that would take people from there directly to his services. For every person who converted, I would get a commission.

The amazing thing is that after setting this up several years ago, I have earned five figures in passive income every single week from this PIV. I was able to create a nice 100 percent passive income stream for myself for a small bit of work I did one time. It's a win for my partner because he generates more business. It's a win for me because I get paid for leveraging my influence and leadership within my community. Most importantly, it's a win for my students because they get customized strategic help for free as they set up one of the most critical and necessary parts of their business.

In fact, you may be reading this book right now and don't yet own an LLC. Or if you do, you will absolutely need to set one up for each new business. So might I suggest you use this company? If that sounds like a good deal to you, visit the link at the end of this chapter to get started. Just a heads-up: I get an affiliate commission if you end up using any of their services in the future (my partnership with them is a perfect example of an affiliate PIV).

See what I did there? I embedded an offer within this book. In fact, if you look closely, you'll see several of them throughout these chapters. The easiest way to find great embedded offers is to simply ask yourself: What do my buyers need next? If it's not something that you sell yourself, go find somebody that does and make a deal with them.

There are more PIVs available today for passivepreneurs than ever before. Check the appendix at the end of the book for a big list. If you want access to even more resources, training, and passive income vehicles I recommend, please visit www.dontstartasidehustle.com/resources.

PART IV

THE WARNINGS

[29]

ABOUT THE WARNINGS

I 'VE HIRED MANY COACHES AND mentors who have been instrumental in helping me get to the next level in my life. Often when I would work with them to lay out a game plan for long-term goals, they would ask me the fun stuff like, "What do you ultimately want? Where do you want to be? What are your dreams? In what time frame do you want to achieve them?"

Once I was all jazzed up about my newly minted dreams, they would ask me to come up with a list of roadblocks, the obstacles that might hold me back from achieving those goals. I would often try to skip over this part of the process. If I have enough desire and drive, I believed, any challenges along the way are going to be irrelevant. I didn't want to focus on the negative; I only wanted to see what was possible. But it was foolish thinking that held me back for years.

The problem with this limiting belief was that whenever a big challenge or setback would happen to me, I was blindsided. Not only was I not expecting it, but I had no plan to overcome the obstacle since I hadn't thought it through in advance. I found myself in the middle of a crisis trying to solve the problem from there. Let me tell you an easier way: come up with a plan in advance for every potential warning.

> No problem can be solved from the same level of consciousness that created it."
>
> **—ALBERT EINSTEIN**

The analogy I like to think about is going to war. When the enemy is about to overrun your position, the time to decide what to do next is *not* when you're being fired at. The proper military strategy would be to lay out every scenario that could happen and make a plan for how to counter each possible attack.

As entrepreneurs, we don't spend a lot of time thinking about defense. We are always looking over the next horizon and thinking about all that we want to achieve. Our heads are in the clouds. That was me. Due to my sheer force of will and desire to keep going despite what happens to me, I was able to have some success. But the setbacks, when they came, would kick my ass.

So I guess the mentors were right after all. I needed to spend as much time becoming aware not only of my weaknesses, but also of the most common warnings. The most powerful result of understanding warnings is that when they happen to us, they're not a surprise. We'll be able to identify which one we are in, and the most effective way to get out of it. Instead of operating from an emotional level of reaction, we'll be operating from a proactive and prepared position.

Many are surprised at the resistance they meet as they move toward their ideal outcome. Because they haven't prepared for the obstacles in advance, they often get derailed. Quitting is the only thing that prevents us from reaching our goal. So the purpose of this segment of the book is to talk about all the scenarios you may experience that will make you want to quit. Once you understand these warnings, you will be better prepared to overcome them. Preparing for the most common pitfalls will give you a huge advantage to prepare for these eventualities. It's not about being negative as some may think, but about being prepared. We shouldn't set out on a journey we've never before taken—not until we've taken stock of everything that could happen along the way.

As we look at each warning, consider how it may have held you back in the past. Make a brutal assessment of whether you are more vulnerable to some of these than to others. Don't fall into the biggest warning of all: believing that you can skip over these warnings. It is the most important process you undertake on your passivepreneur path.

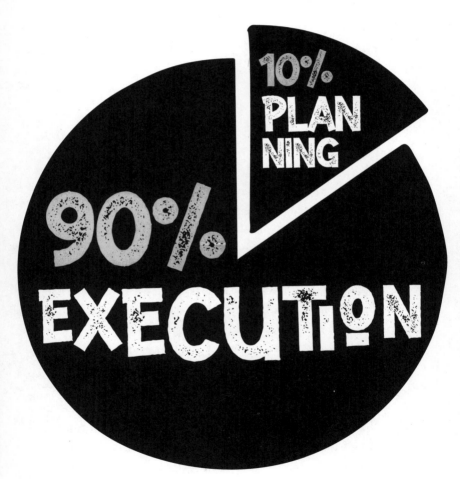

[30]

THE PLANNING WARNING

THIS FIRST WARNING IS ONE of the sneakiest and least recognized pitfalls in wanting to become a passivepreneur. While there is nothing wrong with being prepared, more often than not, people use this activity as an excuse to avoid doing what's difficult. They often use it as a way to avoid their fear of failure. Let me give you an example from my own life.

For over a decade, I wanted to learn how to make money online. I was fascinated by the idea that you could sell digital products to people around the world and make money in your sleep. I determined that I would learn how to do this and become an online marketer myself.

So what did I do? I started preparing. I went out and bought every book I could find on the subject. I set out to learn from the gurus and spent countless hours researching and looking at all the ways to make money online. I went to conferences and got on long phone calls with people who had been successful. I wrote out detailed plans and goals for what I wanted to achieve. I brainstormed ideas and potential ways of getting into the game. And while all these activities were valuable, the thing that I'm embarrassed to admit is that this process went on for ten years. For a decade, I never made a dime online!

It was only after many years of preparation that I was honest with myself. Fear was what was holding me back: fear that I wouldn't be successful and the feeling that I wasn't smart enough to figure it out. So I used preparation as an excuse for delay.

Since preparation is something that doesn't have a concrete end date, it's easy to continue it indefinitely. In my own life, it was only after I decided on a specific action (build a course) and gave myself a time limit to complete it that I made massive progress in this arena. I gave myself three months to produce a finished online course that was ready to sell. After achieving that goal I set out on the second specific action and did that until I achieved my goal of making tens of millions of dollars online.

My belief is that planning and preparing is only 10 percent of the equation. It's necessary but not as critical as you may think. The other 90 percent is executing and taking massive, specific, consistent, daily action toward achieving one's goals.

Again, I can't overemphasize what a huge warning this is for entrepreneurs. Every day I see countless people who would otherwise be successful, who are not even aware that they are caught in the warning of planning. Avoid it like the plague, because the biggest threat of this warning is not even being aware that you're trapped by it!

The most effective way to avoid the planning warning is to set and use deadlines. I get it, deadlines are not sexy. We want to have the freedom to do whatever we want every day. But if we don't have deadlines on a project, procrastination and busyness will fill the gap. So, the most important thing we must apply as a regular habit in our lives is to set a specific completion date for *every* project that we undertake.

Putting time constraints on how we spend our day may sound restrictive, but it creates *more* freedom. That's because we're able to identify when our work begins and ends. It's much easier to reward ourselves for the work that we've done when we know that we've achieved it on schedule. It's also more likely to be completed when we have a deadline.

The next time you have a big project that you want to make huge progress on, by all means, plan out what you're going to do, but keep it brief! Make sure that your planning also has a deadline. We need to move out of the planning phase and into the creation and execution of that plan. Remember: the more you do this, the easier it will be. Planning is essential, but nobody ever planned their way to achievement.

[31]

THE SQUIRREL WARNING

GOT THE NAME FOR THIS warning from the movie *Up*. If you haven't seen the movie, it's about the adventure of an old widower who travels around the world in his flying house. On his journey, he runs across an adorable golden retriever named Dug. Although loving and fiercely loyal, Dug is constantly distracted by squirrels. At random times throughout the movie, Dug will simply freeze and point his nose in one direction and say, "Squirrel!" This dog had an uncontrollable urge to be distracted, as most dogs are when they get the scent of another animal. It was cute and adorable and hilarious to watch throughout the movie, but every time I saw it, I saw myself.

Humans are not all that different. The reason this particular warning is so effective on us is because today there are more opportunities than ever in the history of mankind. It's easy to fall into the warning of becoming an opportunity addict.

The problem with squirrel syndrome is that you never give yourself the gift of focusing on one opportunity long enough to become successful. It's much easier to tell yourself that you found a better opportunity than it is to admit that you've quit. Of all the people I've met in my life, I've never met anyone who honestly admitted that they were a quitter. But we were all quitters at some time in our lives and we quit because we got distracted by the squirrels.

What is the cure for squirrel syndrome? Easy. First, make sure the thing that you've committed to has been done before and that any roadmap you have for achieving it can be trusted. Second, define what success would look like when you get the ideal end result and give yourself a deadline. Finally, you must commit to ignoring all other opportunities until you have achieved that specific goal. That's it.

Once you decide what business you're in, and what your specific outcome is, you must be ruthless about ignoring the squirrels. The interesting thing about the word "decide" is that its suffix, *cide*, is the same suffix of words like "homicide" or "pesticide." *Cide* means to kill or cut off. What if we were to make the word "decide" that powerful? What if when we truly decide, we agree to kill off every other opportunity? What if we murdered even the thought of doing anything else, until we've achieved our predetermined outcome? That, my friend, is the power of deciding, and it is the ultimate antidote to squirrel syndrome.

 Squirrel!"   **−DUG (from the Pixar movie *Up*)**

Here's a newsflash: You can't do everything. You must choose. But the beauty is that in cutting off other options, we free up resources that make success in the one thing we have chosen nearly inevitable. Look at what you've committed yourself to today and decide whether you're willing to cut off all other options until you achieve your goal.

I believe that the only time you should give yourself permission to look at a new opportunity is when you have reached the goal that you set for yourself with the current one. Only then can you decide to move on to something else. The beauty of this approach is that you develop the muscles of completion, focus, and commitment. You will have developed a strong character. Character will carry you through the other warnings and make it much more likely you'll hit the target. *Do not give in to the squirrels.*

[32]

THE PINCHING PENNIES WARNING

ONE THING I'VE NOTICED IS that poor people generally focus on saving money. They use phrases like *squeezing a penny*, *stretching a dollar*, and *making ends meet*. When you are trying to save money, you are in fact telling your mind that there is not enough.

But what I've noticed about super wealthy people is they don't think about any of those things—they're focused on the millions or billions. They only see abundance, making money, acquiring wealth, and creating new streams of income. When you are focused on wealth, you tell your brain there is more than enough. What you focus on in life grows.

> Don't trip over millions to pick up pennies."
>
> **—ME**

I'll give you an example. I was at the beach with my two-year-old daughter last summer. She had her bucket, shovel, and other plastic toys and was thoroughly enjoying our time together. Her favorite activity was to run to the ocean, get her bucket full of seawater, carry it back, and make sand castles. She did this several times until on one waddle back from the ocean, she spilled her bucket of water. She looked at me and immediately burst into tears. "I spilled all my water, Dada!" She was nearly inconsolable.

I picked her up and hugged her and walked her back to the ocean. I pointed out to the horizon so she could see. "Honey, look at all this water. It's more than you can ever put in your bucket for the rest of your life. Don't worry about the water you lost, baby. We can go get as much as you want right now."

It's understandable why a toddler would think this way, but as adults we think this way too—about money. We believe that money is limited. Sadly we only believe this because it has been our experience for most of our lives that money is scarce. We are on the beach facing the wrong way, trying to scrape a bucketful of cash out of the wet sand when behind us is an ocean of money.

Here's the truth: when you treat money as though it's scarce, you will take actions based on that belief that lead to more scarcity. You will find ways to spend less and save, but you won't have the energy—or even awareness—to see the opportunities right in front of you. You will spill the only bucket you have!

A mentor of mine once told me about his beliefs around wealth. Every day he would wake up and say out loud, "Making millions is easy." Now that might sound offensive to you. It sounded offensive to me when I first heard it—but he had that belief. The only reason that it sounded threatening to me was because it goes against everything that I believed about money at the time. How could making millions be easy?

But I decided to try his experiment. Every day I'd wake up, look in the mirror, and shout, "Making millions is easy!" I looked like an idiot. But I stuck to it. I repeated it to myself so many times that I believed it in my core. I remember telling people that this was my new belief now and they thought I was crazy. I may have looked like an idiot, but soon enough, I was a rich idiot! Avoid the warning of pinching pennies; it will keep you poor for the rest of your life.

How do we do this? Here's what I suggest. Rather than asking questions like, "How can I save money on groceries this week?" or "Where can I buy the cheapest gas to fill up my car?" ask these questions instead: "How can I make my next million dollars?" or "How can I double my money in the next thirty days?" or as my boy Grant Cardone likes to say, "How can I earn ten times my income?" After all, if you were to increase your income by 1,000 percent in the next year, would you care about the price of groceries or how to save on gas? Nope. The right questions create wealth but the wrong ones compound poverty.

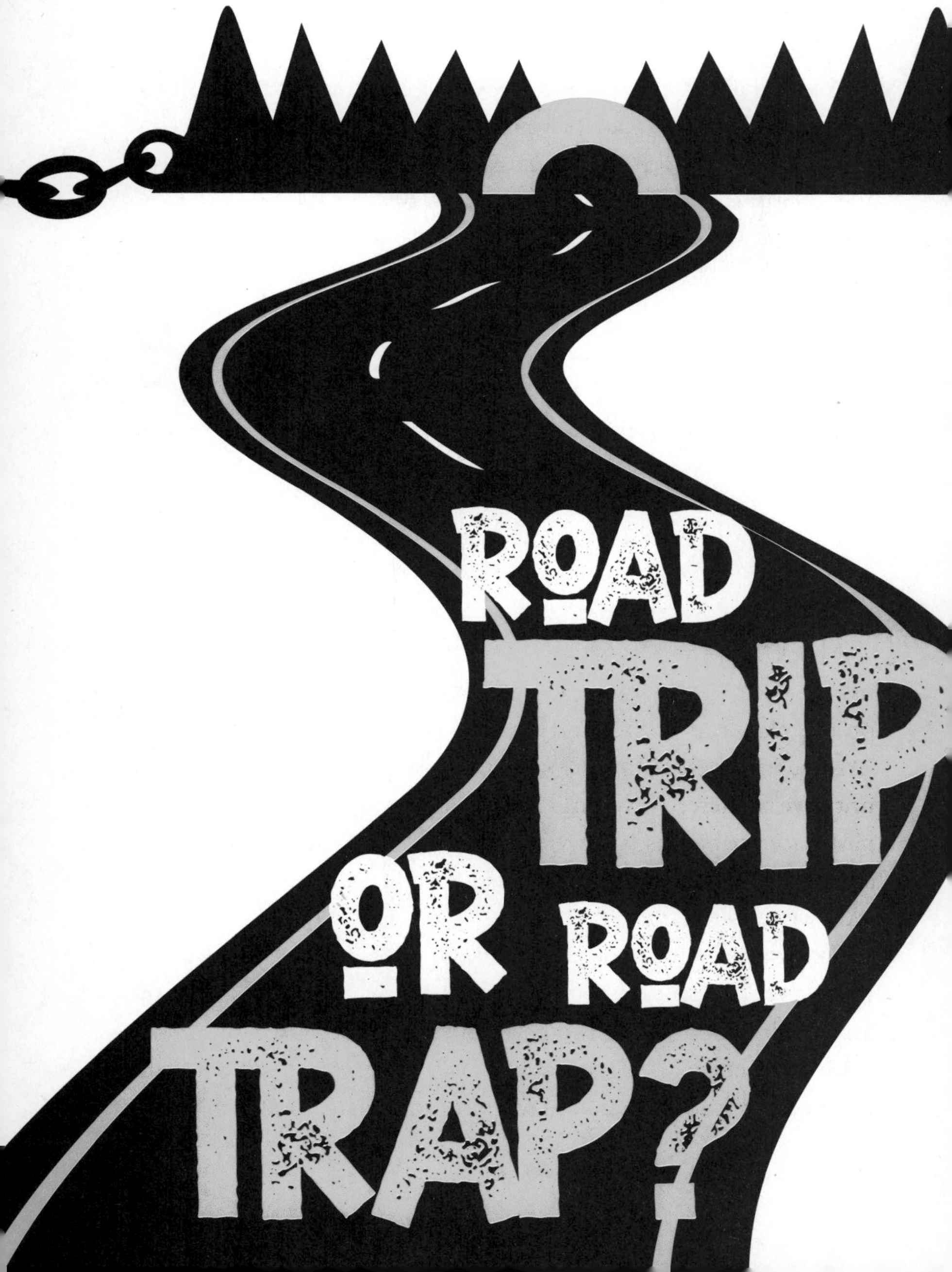
ROAD TRIP
OR ROAD
TRAP?

[33]

THE ROAD-TRIP WARNING

MY DAD'S CHEVY STATION WAGON was a beige land barge with faux-wood paneling, three rows of bench seating, and a rear window that rolled down.

On long trips, my sister and I would pass the time by flopping over the tops of the seats, fighting with each other about who would get which row—with the winner getting to stay in the "way, way back" where we would make faces at the drivers of cars behind us. We went on a lot of trips as a family, and like all the other kids on the planet, my sister and I would incessantly ask my parents, "Are we there yet? When are we gonna get there? How much longer until we're there?" Over and over and over again. Children don't have patience because they're immature, but it's also true that many adults are immature. Just like kids, they keep asking themselves, "Are we there yet, Dad?"

The road-trip warning is about being impatient for the destination. It's about putting your focus on the fact that you haven't yet arrived. It's about being too hard on yourself because you haven't achieved your goal. What's fascinating is that when you let go of the need to know when you're going to arrive, you often arrive much sooner. Best of all, you get to enjoy the journey. It's much better to be pleasantly surprised when you arrive early than to be disappointed and frustrated because things aren't going fast enough.

If we want to achieve our goal by a specific date, and we get to that date and it hasn't happened yet, we have to know that it will happen in due time. We aren't going to quit simply because the timeline needs to be adjusted. Often, the journey happens slower than we anticipated, but that should have no bearing on our emotional state today. We have to be content being in the very back row of our business, trusting that we will arrive at our destination.

It was only when my sister and I forgot about where we were going and enjoyed the ride that time seemed to fly by. Let us not get tripped up by the road-trip warning, or we risk completely missing the journey that we're on.

So what's the cure for the road-trip warning? Patience. It's an old-fashioned word that few of us can say we practice. The fire that gives us a burning desire to succeed in life and business often seems like the opposite of patience. How can we be patient when we have so much ambition and such big dreams? Won't being patient slow our progress? No, quite the opposite. When we learn to enjoy each step and we know in our soul that we will arrive when we are supposed to arrive, we can enjoy a lot more of the journey.

I've been guilty of lacking patience at many points in my life. I would find myself so forcefully pushing forward with my quest to become successful that I would lose all the joy in the day-to-day. It took a friend to wake me up a little bit. She said something to me that I found profound at the time:

"If the Brian from a decade ago were to meet the Brian you are today, he would be shocked by what you've been able to achieve." That woke me up. What if, today, I was already be a hero to my past self? What if I was measuring my present self by bigger and bigger goals in my future, goals that were making me feel like I had so far to go? What if I could stop and congratulate myself on all that had happened up until this point, by looking at it through the eyes of who I was a few years ago? It's a powerful perspective that has served me ever since.

Avoid the road-trip warning. This trip is supposed to be fun!

[34]

THE CAUSE-AND-EFFECT WARNING

WE ALL WANT TO HAVE six-pack abs and a toned body without ever having to go to the gym. That's why an entire industry has sprung up to sell us that promise. We want to be able to lose weight without giving up any of the foods that we like. Enter the diet industry. We also want to become wealthy with no real effort on our part. Again, there are plenty of people who will make us believe that this is possible.

We desire the effect—that's what we're after—but we're not willing to consider the cause that makes that effect possible. We want something for nothing. Not only do we want something for nothing, but we want it *now*. We often fail to understand that our actions today will have a slight impact on tomorrow. But actions taken every single day over a long time will have a huge impact on our future.

A mentor once asked me a simple question: "Would you be willing to put in two years of full-time intense work with no pay with the guarantee that you would make millions of dollars at the end of those two years?" The answer was heck yeah, I was willing to do that. But the thing about entrepreneurship is, you aren't sure if you're going to get that result. So, by being unsure that the effect will happen, we don't create the cause required to make it inevitable.

Here's my challenge to you so you avoid this warning. It involves, wait for it, another question. Are you willing to pay the price? Are you willing to do whatever it takes with little reward or positive feedback, if you know that you will break through and be successful? Most can't answer yes to that question—and that's when they quit. They're not willing to pay the price.

I remember working between six months and two years on every business I started, but not one of them made money immediately. I began with the mindset that I was willing to do whatever it took and become whomever I needed to be (cause) to see success (effect). I didn't care how long it took.

To be prepared to sidestep this all-too-common warning, we need to develop delayed gratification; it's a hallmark of maturity. The ability to delay gratification is a quality that adults possess, and children do not. Children expect to get what they want the moment they demand it. As a parent I can tell you, it's one of the more annoying things about kids. We try to explain to our children that just because they demand it doesn't mean they will receive it. We understand this as adults, but often fail to recognize that we can act like children ourselves. Like Veruca Salt in *Charlie and the Chocolate Factory,* we want what we want, and we want it now! We expect that if we do this, we will get that, and as if that weren't enough, it should happen in the time frame we planned on!

Imagine if we could put in the necessary work knowing that we might not see the fruits of that work for a while. It may appear that nothing is happening when we are in fact building massive momentum.

I saw an interview recently with a well-known Hollywood star. The interviewer asked her what it's like to be an overnight success.

This starlet looked at the interviewer a bit puzzled. Her response was pointed. "I'm not an overnight success. I've been working on my craft for fourteen years. I've taken minor rolls and crap work where I could get it for most of my life. I've gone on hundreds if not thousands of auditions where I've been rejected for roles. I've never had more than $1,000 in my bank account until a year ago and I've never complained about any of it because of my love of the craft. I never set out to even become famous. So to say that I'm an overnight success is not accurate. I've always been successful. I'm just now finally being recognized for it."

[35]

THE INDIFFERENCE
WARNING

THERE'S A STORY ABOUT SOCRATES and one of his students. The student approached the wise teacher and asked him for the secret to all knowledge. Socrates replied, "I will teach you," and led him to a river. He waded out into the water and asked his student to follow him. When the young pupil waded out into the chest-high water, Socrates grabbed him forcefully by his hair and shoved him under the water. The boy struggled violently to get away, clawing and pushing to get above the surface. But Socrates, with his iron grip, had more strength than the boy and kept him firmly under the water. After nearly a minute of struggle, the boy began to fear for his life. He believed that he would die if he didn't find a way to escape. Right at the point where the boy was about to lose all his strength and give up, Socrates pulled him out of the water. He released the boy as he gasped for air. The teacher walked him to shore and gently sat him down. He looked at his student and revealed, "When you want knowledge as badly as you want your next breath, you will find it."

When a lack of true desire takes hold of a person, they don't find the fuel they need to continue through the inevitable difficulties that lie ahead. As Napoleon Hill states in his book *Think and Grow Rich*, "a burning desire" is a prerequisite to achievement. A good way to think about desire is like a thermostat. If you set your thermostat to seventy degrees in the winter, your house will never get warmer than that temperature. To make the house warmer, you must reset the thermostat to a higher degree. Only then does everything in that environment have to meet the new threshold. Many of us have our thermostat turned off and don't understand why we are freezing. You have to raise your level of desire to raise your results. You must raise your minimum temperature so that you never again fall below it.

Often, we have only a vague wish for something, but not a burning, all-consuming desire. We slip into indifference, where we think it would be nice to achieve something, but we don't feel too strongly about it. But instead of thinking, "That would be nice," we must say, "I will do whatever it takes, right now, and forever." To avoid this pitfall, it's critical that you develop an unreasonable desire for success. Desire success as you would desire oxygen when being held underwater. You no longer want; you desperately need. That is the power of desire and the number-one killer of indifference.

I believe the most effective way to turn our wants into burning desires is to vividly imagine what it would be like to achieve them. For example, let's say you want to buy your dream house. It's one thing to write that as a goal, but it's an entirely different thing to vividly imagine what it would be like to open the door to that new house, to breathe in the scent of the front foyer, to hear the sound your shoes make on the marble floor as your steps echo through the two-story entryway. To vividly live out that experience in advance would create much more desire for that goal than if you were to be lukewarm about it. Heck, imagine if you were to ask a realtor to give you a tour of that dream house so you could experience it in person. Now we're talking! Do whatever it takes to increase your desire and you will avoid this all-too-common trap.

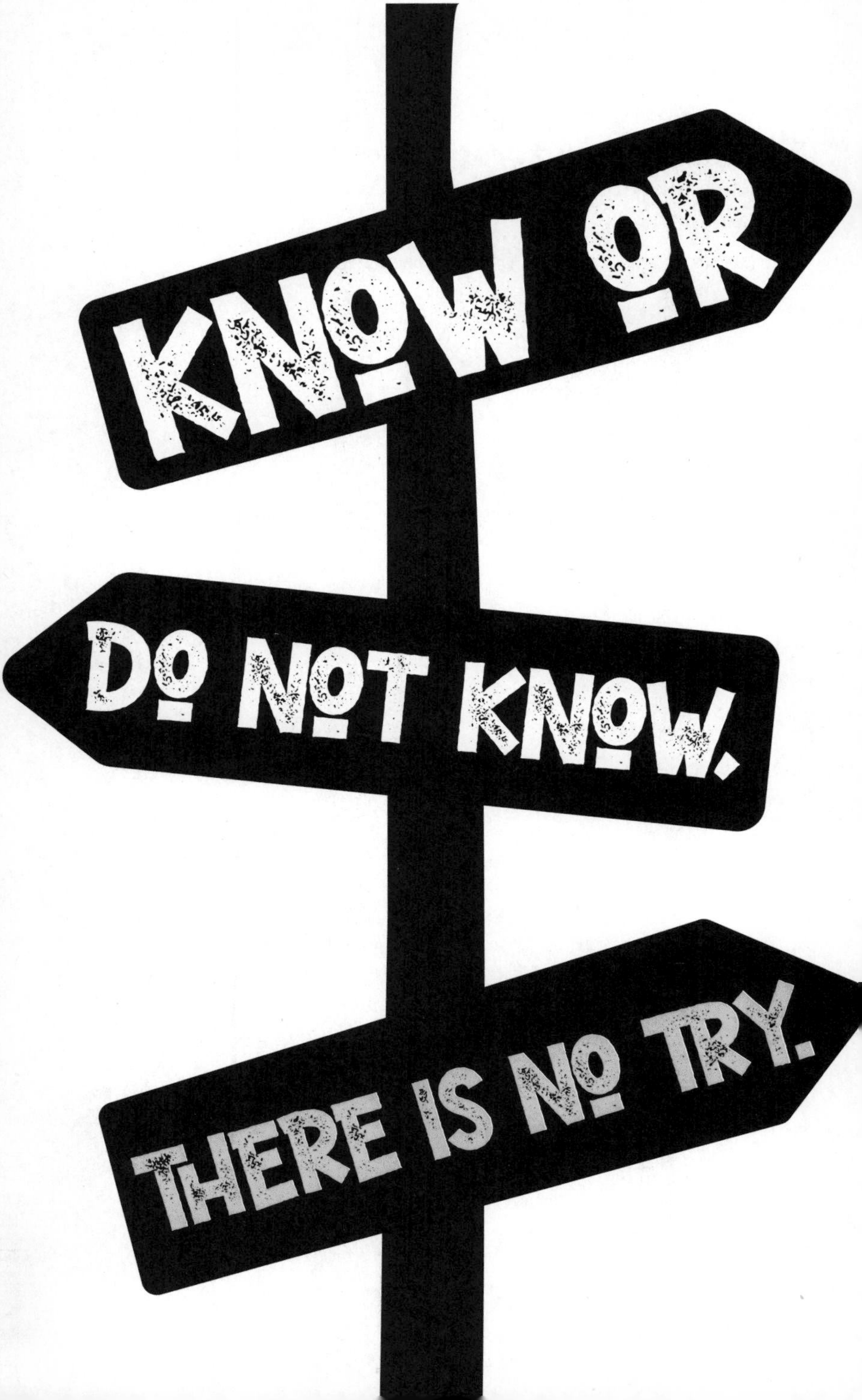
KNOW OR
DO NOT KNOW.
THERE IS NO TRY.

[36]

THE IGNORANCE WARNING

THE EXCUSE THAT MANY PEOPLE use to avoid achieving what they most desire in life is simply this: "I don't know how." What's amazing about the ignorance warning is that everybody who has ever lived would be justified in using it. I mean who is born knowing how to do things? Babies know how to crap, suck, and scream. Everything else is learned. That baby shows up in the world with no skills or knowledge.

Every single person starts at the same point, which is knowing nothing. If you understand that at a gut level, you will see that we all are in the same boat. The good news is that most anything you want to learn can in fact be learned. For some of us it will be easier than for others, but with enough time and effort, we can know how to do anything.

"I don't know how" is an easy excuse to get out of taking action. It's a way out because it assumes one doesn't have the ability to learn. You should avoid it. Today we live in the information age. The amount of information and education that we have access to is unprecedented in human history. Not only is the volume of information infinitely larger than at any time in the past, but the access to information is also unlimited. With an internet connection, most people have at their fingertips the whole of human knowledge from anywhere in the world. In fact, Google is in the process of digitizing every single published book and making them available online. We can hear lectures and training from experts in any field and we can watch YouTube and see visual demonstrations of how to do specific tasks. We can access highly specialized education courses, books, and training—all with a simple search. Stop saying you don't know how.

Here's a simple statement you should tattoo on your forehead if you suffer from this warning: "I have the ability to figure it out." Let me give you an example from my own life. Early on when I was trying to figure out how to make money online, it seemed like every time I turned around, there was some new skill set that I had to learn. I had to set up a merchant account, learn what SEO was, build a sales funnel, write copy, create an offer, build a course, and be good at presenting on video. I had to have some understanding of branding and product design, hiring and firing, working with teams, delegating—and the list goes on. It was overwhelming, but I found a hack that seemed to work well.

When I didn't know how to do something, I had two options. The first one was to learn how to do it myself. But the downside was I was limited on how much time I had; I didn't have the time to learn every one of those skill sets.

The second option was to find others who already had that skill set. I came to the realization that I didn't need to know everything. I didn't fall into the pit of feeling that I had to master everything. I realized that the access I had to information was also an access to people who had expertise.

Today you can go online to websites like Fiverr or Upwork and for $5 an hour hire freelancers in Asia who have master's degrees. You can hire someone with a doctorate in India for less than what your barista makes at Starbucks. There is an overwhelming supply of human capital, and people who are gladly willing and able to help. They can assist you with anything that you need help with for a nominal amount of money.

I get asked questions about my business all the time that I don't know how to answer. People will ask me specifics about my sales funnel or how to write great copy, or how to edit beautiful sales videos, and I will answer that I don't know—because I didn't create them. Instead, I found the best people that I could afford to do that work for me. That may sound like ignorance, but it's selective ignorance.

One of my heroes was Henry Ford. It was said that he wasn't the most intelligent man in the world, and the local newspapers accused him of that many times. In one interview, as the reporter attempted to trap him with obscure questions, Ford replied to the question with another. "Why would I need to know those things when I could pick up the phone and ask anybody in my organization to get the answer for me?" He understood the power of staying in his lane. He knew he didn't need to know how to think for himself if he could find the people who did.

[37]

THE "NOT ENOUGH TIME" WARNING

"**I DON'T HAVE THE TIME." PEOPLE** step into this big, steaming pile of crap excuse *all the time*. I've got a newsflash for you. Nobody has the time. Unless you're retired, or already independently wealthy, or sitting in prison, no one wakes up in the morning with nothing to do.

The difference between those who do and those who don't is this: those who have the time *have made the time*. There are so many activities throughout the average American's day that are optional. Many of us are not aware of how many times we glance at our phone or look at social media. We don't take stock of how many hours per week, or even hours per night, we spend bingeing on Netflix or watching TV. We don't consider the possibility of waking up an hour or two earlier, God forbid, to make our dreams a reality. We choose not to listen to audiobooks in our car on the way to work or study up during our lunch break. We almost never turn our phones on airplane mode for the few hours that we have carved out to build our business. We haven't been ruthless with creating the time necessary to achieve our dreams.

Here's how I found the time in my own life. I sat down one night and looked at all the places that I was spending my time outside of my job. I made a list of all kinds of things, like time spent on social media, streaming my favorite shows, and when I was single, going out to meet girls. I spent time socializing and planning events or going to the beach or out on a boat for the day. I liked to read the news endlessly. There were a million and one things I did that took up all my time between work and sleep. I wrote them all down.

Once I had my list, I circled every single thing that I was willing to give up in exchange for a million dollars. The only thing I didn't cross off the list was eating, but I did cross off eating out. I became pretty extreme with cutting out all the extras in my life so I could carve out time.

One of the things that I thought would be imperative was to make it difficult to fall back into my old habits. Generally, when I got home from work, I would eat dinner and then drift to the couch where I would watch TV for the rest of the evening. That's why I decided the only way I could ensure this didn't happen was not only to cancel my Netflix account but put my TV in the attic! I unplugged my flat-screen, went upstairs, and laid it in the corner under a blanket. I decided that I would not watch TV again until I had made a million dollars. To get even more extreme, I told myself I didn't deserve to watch TV again until I hit that goal. I was putting limits on Brian this time! Was it worth it? Yes! Would it have happened without me being so extreme? No, I don't think so.

It was not easy. There were many times when I went to fill the time with what I used to do in the evening, only to find that the TV was not there. Every time I did that, it was a reminder that I needed to get to work. I would often work on my side business at 9:00 or 10:00 p.m. for the couple hours that I would have wasted away with mindless entertainment.

The powerful result is that all the minutes and hours I saved were freed up to be directly channeled into my business. I'm not special. I was willing to pay the price of not having what I wanted, right now, to drive me toward my goal. I made myself uncomfortable with the idea that discomfort would push me even harder. So my question to you is: Do you truly not have the time?

FORGET

THE HUSTLE

AND FOCUS

ON FLOW.

[38]

THE SIDE-HUSTLE WARNING

A **FEW MONTHS AGO I LANDED** in Orlando for a business conference. After I grabbed my luggage, I walked outside to catch my Uber. Within a few minutes, a blue Toyota Camry rolled up and a well-dressed guy in his mid-thirties stepped out and asked, "Hey, are you Brian? I'm Jason." Without hesitating, he dropped my overweight suitcase in the trunk and invited me to take a seat. As we exited the airport toward the highway, we made small talk about the sweltering Florida humidity and I told him why I was in town. The conversation turned to work and I asked him whether or not driving was his full-time gig. He said he had been working in an office nine to five for several years but needed a change. Being able to start and end his day whenever he wanted and not having a boss was what attracted him to Uber.

I wanted to help him, so I asked a very simple question. "Jason, would it be possible for you to make ten times more next year driving for Uber?" He didn't say anything for a bit. "That would be awesome, but no." He laughed. "I don't know any way to do that, but I do know if I work around the clock six or seven days a week, I could maybe bring in as much as $70,000 this year, which isn't bad."

"That's great," I said. "I get that driving for Uber gives you more freedom than the job that you left, but where is this thing ultimately going to take you? What if there was a way to make great money without hustling constantly? What would you do with your time if you weren't always on the road?"

He looked at me a bit confused. "Okay, what are you suggesting I do?"

"I suggest that you keep driving Uber while you find a source of passive or semipassive income," I replied. "Over time, you can reduce the number of hours that you drive so you can invest even more time into building something that will sustain you later. The great news is that you have such flexibility with Uber that you can easily do both. I can show you how to stack passive income sources so you'll never again need a side hustle."

He politely nodded with his eyes still on the road as his phone dinged. He seemed to be much more concerned about the new ride request on his phone than the potentially life-altering advice I was sharing with him. Twenty minutes later he dropped me at the hotel and I thanked him as I got my luggage. As he drove away, I couldn't help but think about a much, much bigger world that he could be playing in—but not one he'll ever get to enjoy until he finds a way to escape his gig mentality.

By definition, side hustles are really any way of making money over and above what one does for their main source of income. But if your "day job" pays well enough, why would you need a side gig? They are an income Band-Aid at best. My favorite kind of income is the kind that comes in whether I'm hustling or not.

Let's not forget that a side hustle is fully reliant on the one doing the hard work. It's not scalable. It does not have unlimited potential earnings. It can't be automated since it is 100 percent reliant on one's own efforts. What is a side hustle really? It's just a fancy way of saying "second job."

There's one more really big thing that riles me up about side hustles. The company that provides the hustle has two products they are selling. First, they sell the service—like a hot meal delivered to your front door, or a ride from Point A to Point B. But what they also sell is the opportunity. Without the opportunity, they can't recruit millions of gig workers that make the machine work. Either way, gig companies become very good at sucking in consumers (and gig workers, aka side hustlers) who all contribute to making the founders of that company very, very rich. Those who sign up for side hustles work for those who've created them!

Side hustles, over the long term, become the exact opposite of what it means to be a passivepreneur. Being a passivepreneur isn't about more cash, it's about cash flow. It's not about working hard, it's about working less. A side hustle is really just a job you own. It's the illusion of freedom, but it is far from what we need to become truly free. A side hustle should be merely a brief stopover on the way to passivepreneurship, not the destination.

When you really understand how to stack PIVs, it becomes even more clear why I tell you not to start a side hustle. Stacking does not rely on you long term, and it allows you to sleep at night knowing that you have income redundancy. The best part is, the more PIVs you set up, the more likely that one of them will be a runaway hit, the kind of opportunity that can make you insanely rich. For those reasons and more, ditch the side hustle and instead become a passivepreneur.

CON
CLU
SION.

[CONCLUSION]

I BELIEVE THAT WITH A few years of concentrated effort applied to building passive income, you can set yourself up to be free for life. The result will be not just having what you want materially, but also what you need spiritually, mentally, and emotionally.

Decide now that you will do whatever it takes for as long as it takes to become a passivepreneur, even if the results don't come quickly. Stop believing that there's a limit on what you can earn or that you have to give away the rest of your life for money. Decide that you will not fall prey to the warnings we covered in this book and that you will be prepared for them when they arise.

You now have all that you need for the journey. Any one of these ideas, if executed properly, can change your life. Believe that people and events will align and even conspire to help you succeed. Opportunities will open up to you and others will stand in amazement as you go from breakthrough to breakthrough. Let's hope one day our paths will cross so you can tell me all about it.

Life is short and your time is precious. Thank you for spending it here with me in this book.

Your Biggest Fan,
Brian

ADDITIONAL RESOURCES

There is so much in this book that will help you take the next step toward becoming a passivepreneur. Beyond what you find in this book, though, I also want to give you access to more resources that will help you on your journey. The best way to keep those resources up to date is to put them on a site where I can update them regularly. I've compiled a list of PIVs I recommend, case studies of successful passivepreneurs, PDF downloads, and more. To access everything, simply go to www.dontstartasidehustle.com/resources. Enjoy!

[ACKNOWLEDGMENTS]

I HAD NO IDEA WHEN I started this journey what an undertaking it is to write a book. This project would not have happened without those who supported me during this process and through the years.

Thank you, Steven Snyder, for teaching me most of what I know about copywriting, marketing, and offers. You've been my secret weapon behind the scenes and instrumental to my first big win online. Keep noodling.

I'm forever grateful to Mohammed Ali, one of the wisest people I have ever known. You are forever adding value to my life and have pushed me to think bigger than I find comfortable. Thank you, my dear friend.

To my BNB Formula team, you are family. Thank you to Brad Brandon, the one-man sales machine at BNBF—I love you, brother. Diane Spotts, who never takes a break even though I ask her to every week. Ryan Garnhum, you keep the machine running smoothly every day and have never once let me down. Kristen Hayse, the best affiliate manager in the world. Thank you for bringing in millions right from day one and being my best promoter. Blake Nubar, you were there in the earliest days and are now one of my best friends. I know you forever "bleed BNB," and you are truly a gem, brother.

Thank you to the entire 2 Market Media team: Grazi Mirabile, Mercedes Randall, Ally Walsh, Hank Norman, and so many others. Colin Murray, Michelle Rose, and the entire team at Jump 450. To every single person who's ever promoted my offers and given me the honor of presenting to their lists, thank you!

A very special thanks to Steve Carlis, who paved the way for me to get this book done. I can't even take credit for the idea of being an author because it started with you. Thank you.

For Akbar Sheikh, who helped me when I was clueless about how to make my first dollar online and who has the most generous heart. Brent Smith, who taught me how to let go of the outcome, how to be the mayor and ultimately change my story. Thank you, Steve Harward—you are the most connected and genuine business badass I know. Thank you also to Paul Getter and James Starr, the coolest internet marketing nerds I know.

A very, very special thank-you to the leadership and entire sales team at Apex. You are not only world-class, you are also now the best in the world. To Caleb Maddix and Ryan O'Donnell who lead this team of winners, thank you for adding rocket fuel to BNB Formula and for inspiring me every day with your passion for life and business.

To the very best client advisors on the planet: thank you to the entire Apex and IO Consortium teams. A special thanks to Stefan Fincias and Mallory Gold. Caleb Maddix and Ryan O'Donnell, you guys are way too young to be so successful. Thank you for bringing more passion and energy to the cause than I ever could. Ten a month, here we come!

This book is especially in honor of my BNB coaching team. You guys bring the true value to our community every single day, and I consider every one of you a friend. Thank you, Brad Dillard, Hal Wilkerson, Justin Qualkenbush, Alex Jarbo, Ari Ymy, and the real boss, Sue Jordan, who never misses a single call, even if she has to show up in her robe.

To everyone at HarperCollins Leadership, Dupree Miller, and the editing team who collectively taught me on the fly how to write a book. Thank you, Jan Miller, Sara Kendrick, Ali Kominsky, Lolly

Spindler, Arestia Rosenberg, and Linda Alila. Literally would not be literary without you.

To Mom, it's been quite a year, but we're still here. Your belief in me is to this day stronger than my own belief in myself. You're still my favorite mom. To Matt, Emerson, Parker, and Silas: I love you guys. And to Liz, who is at least twice the writer on her worst day than I will ever be.

A very special thank-you to my love and beautiful bride, Janielly. If we have nothing in this world, the blessing of our little family makes us the richest people on Earth. To my baby girls, Julia and Abbi. I know this book will never be *Llama Llama* and you can't read it yet, but I love you nuggets more than you'll ever know.

Finally, to all those who have been a part of my journey so far. My mentors, partners, trailblazers, and friends . . . Tai Lopez, Grant Cardone, Roland Frasier, Dominic Hrabe, Kelly Gannon, Holly Flick, James Starr, Paul Getter, Emily Rhem, Tim Bratz, Brandan Fisher, Chris Daigle, Mike Dillard, Braydon Ross, Russell Cox, Dustin Crooks, Karen King, Gregory Wexler, Patrick Riddle, Pete Vargas, Grant Cardone, Frank Kern, Dean Graziosi, Dave Galagar, Jerry Conti, Russell Brunson, Tony Robbins, and Tim Ferriss. Thank you!

Ultimately, I give all credit to Jesus Christ, who is not only the bestselling author of all time, but the only one who can offer riches that last forever.

[APPENDIX]

LIST OF PIVS

Owner—PIVs You Purchase

- Dividend stocks and bonds
- Residential and commercial real estate
- Real estate syndication and REITs
- Commercial real estate funds
- Intellectual property: patents, domains, trademarks, data, copyrights
- Automated businesses: parking lots, vending machines, laundromats, car washes, billboards
- Insurance annuities
- Existing businesses with management in place
- Limited business partnerships
- Infinite banking
- Crypto staking, mining, and yield farming

Creator—PIVs You Create

- Create an online course and charge subscription fee
- Blogging (up-front effort), but email list becomes an asset
- Write an e-book or traditional book
- Apps or Alexa skill
- Sell photography (post to stock image sites for purchase)
- Photography or video content creation
- Start a podcast (some active)
- Create software (somewhat active—but then license)

- Instagram- or TikTok-sponsored posts
- Content creator or influencer
- License music
- Sell digital design files (on sites like Etsy)
- Memberships, subscriptions, and member-only content
- Branded sponsorships
- NFTs

Controller—PIVs You Share or Control

- Homesharing: Airbnb, VRBO, Homeaway
- Affiliate marketing
- Drop shipping, private labeling, and print on demand
- Retail arbitrage: buying at one price from brick and mortar and selling at a higher price online
- Rent unused space (for example, a shed or garage to neighbors)
- Rent useful household items (tools, lawn mowers, camping equipment)
- Sharing economy: carshare, RV share, boatshare, poolshare!
- Vehicle advertising
- Reverse mortgages
- Network marketing, direct sales, and multilevel marketing
- Peer-to-peer lending, crowdfunding, seed funding, and micro lending
- Brand sponsorships, partnerships, and collaborations
- Amazon and Facebook stores
- Automated trucking
- Youtube monetization businesses

For additional tools, trainings, and ideas, please visit www.dontstartasidehustle.com.

[NOTES]

Chapter 1

1. Zack Friedman, "50% of Millennials Are Moving Back Home with Their Parents After College," *Forbes*, June 6, 2019, https://www.forbes.com/sites/zackfriedman/2019/06/06/millennials-move-back-home-college/?sh=98fd042638ad.
2. Elsie Chen, "These Chinese Millennials Are 'Chilling,' and Beijing Isn't Happy," *New York Times*, October 10, 2021, https://www.nytimes.com/2021/07/03/world/asia/china-slackers-tangping.html.
3. Donald Sull, Charles Sull, and Ben Zweig, "Toxic Culture Is Driving the Great Resignation," *MIT Sloan Management Review*, January 11, 2022, https://sloanreview.mit.edu/article/toxic-culture-is-driving-the-great-resignation/.
4. Marcus Lu, "These 3 Studies Point to the Mental Health Benefits of Working Less," World Economic Forum, February 19, 2020, https://www.weforum.org/agenda/2020/02/shorter-workweek-people-happier/.
5. Elle Hunt, "Japan's Karoshi Culture Was a Warning. We Didn't Listen," *WIRED*, February 6, 2021, https://www.wired.co.uk/article/karoshi-japan-overwork-culture.
6. Kari Paul, "Microsoft Japan Tested a Four-Day Work Week and Productivity Jumped by 40%," *The Guardian*, November 4, 2019, https://www.theguardian.com/technology/2019/nov/04/microsoft-japan-four-day-work-week-productivity.

Chapter 12

1. Michelle Fox, "Out of Work and Desperate: Here's What College Graduates Are Facing and What They Can Do About It," CNBC, April 15, 2021, https://www.cnbc.com/2021/04/15/what-college-graduates-can-do-about-being-out-of-work.html.
2. Brad Plumer, "Only 27 Percent of College Grads Have a Job Related to Their Major," *Washington Post*, May 20, 2013, https://www

.washingtonpost.com/news/wonk/wp/2013/05/20/only-27-percent
-of-college-grads-have-a-job-related-to-their-major/.

3. Elizabeth Redden, "41% of Recent Grads Work in Jobs Not
Requiring a Degree," Inside Higher Ed, February 18, 2020, https://
www.insidehighered.com/quicktakes/2020/02/18/41-recent-grads
-work-jobs-not-requiring-degree.

4. Melanie Hanson, "Student Loan Default Rate," Education Data
Initiative, December 19, 2021, https://educationdata.org/student
-loan-default-rate#:~:text=An%20average%20of%2015%25%20
of,loans%20enter%20default%20each%20year; Melanie Hanson,
"Student Loan Debt Statistics," Education Data Initiative, March 1,
2022, https://educationdata.org/student-loan-debt-statistics.

[INDEX]

[ABOUT THE AUTHOR]

BRIAN PAGE is a writer, speaker, and award-winning educator focused on habit creation, entrepreneurship, and personal growth. He is the host of the *Digital Titans* podcast, founder of the Page Fund, and star of the reality show *House Hackers*. As creator of the world's #1 bestselling Airbnb training, The BNB Formula, he has taught more than one hundred thousand students in forty-seven countries. Page has worked with such heavyweights as Kevin Harrington from *Shark Tank*, Tai Lopez, Dean Graziosi, and Grant Cardone, and has been featured in *Inc.*, *Entrepreneur*, and *Forbes*, and on MSNBC. For speaking engagements and to learn more, please visit www.brian.page.